My Big Book of Writing
Learn to Write the Uppercase and Lowercase Alphabet

Copyright © 2020 Vernada Thomas.

All rights reserved.

No portion of this book may be reproduced, stored in a retrieval system, or transmitted in any form or by any means without prior written permission of publishers.

ISBN-10: 0991244303
ISBN-13: 978-0-9912-4430-0

Aa

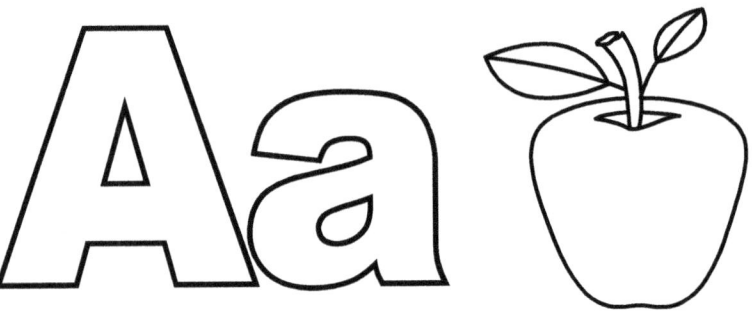

A is for apple.
Trace the uppercase A and lowercase a. Color the letters and the pictures.

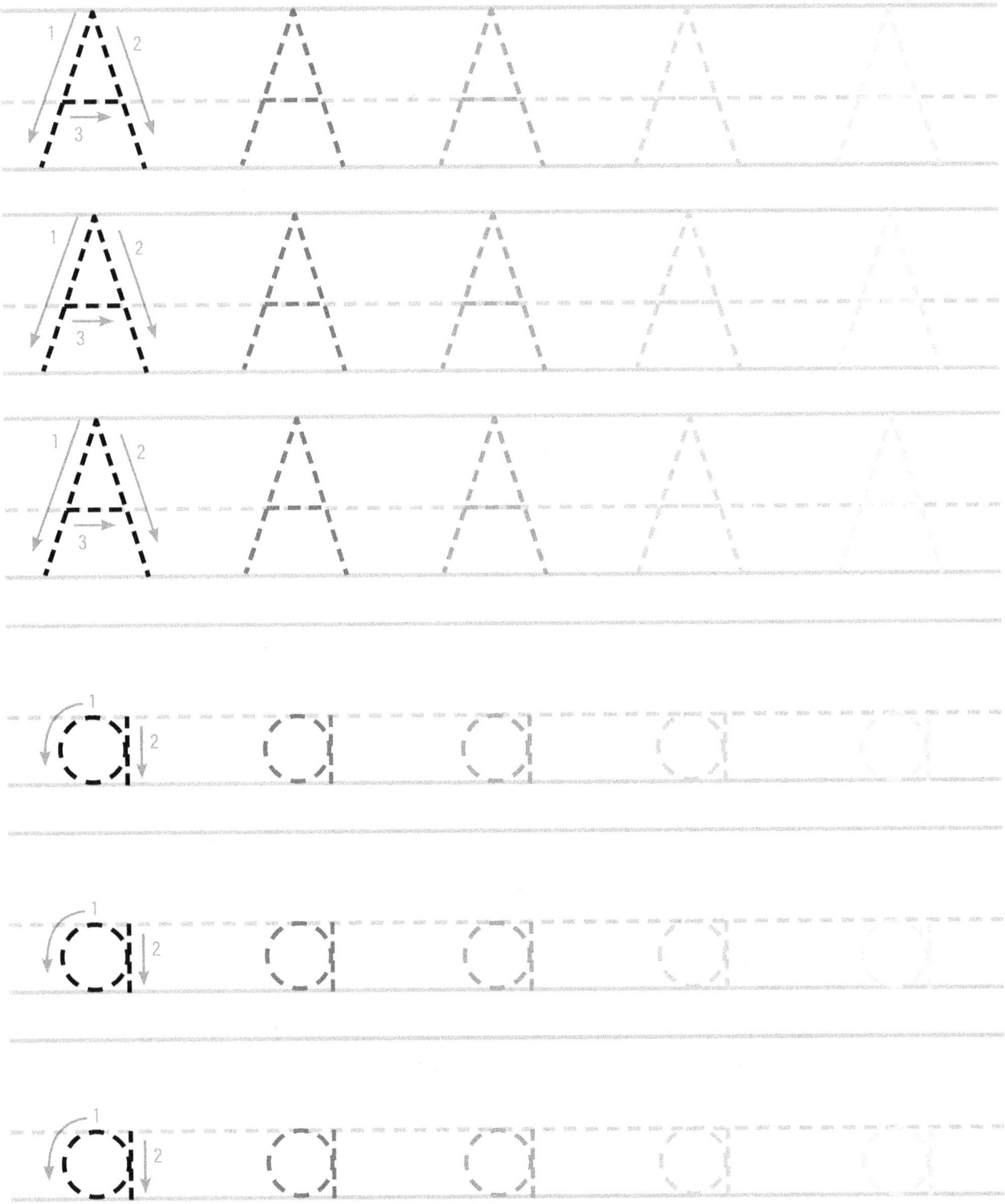

A is for acorn.
Count the acorn below. How many do you count? Write the number here:

Can you say the number 1 out loud?

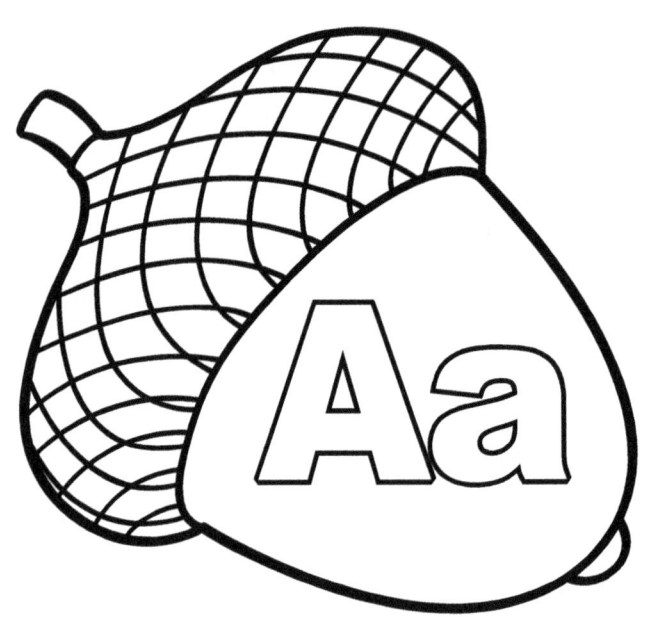

Practice writing the number 1 and one.

Practice writing the number 1 and one.

Bb

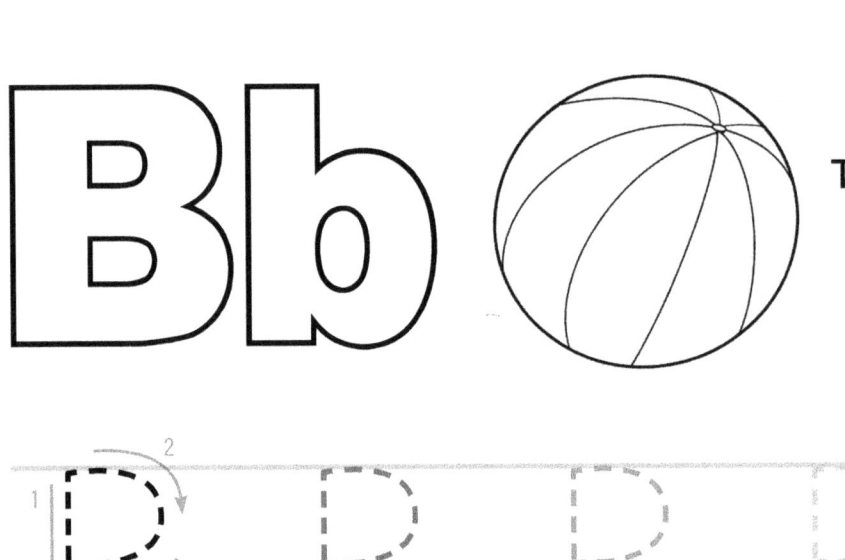

B is for ball.
Trace the uppercase B and lowercase b.
Color the letters and the pictures.

B B B B B

B B B B B

B B B B B

b b b b b

b b b b b

b b b b b

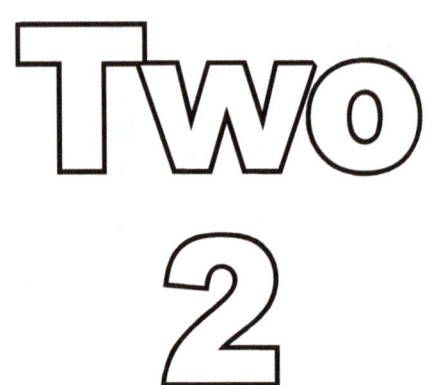

B is for bats.
Count the bats below. How many do you count? Write the number here:

Can you say the number 2 out loud?

Practice writing the number 2 and two.

Practice writing the number 2 and two.

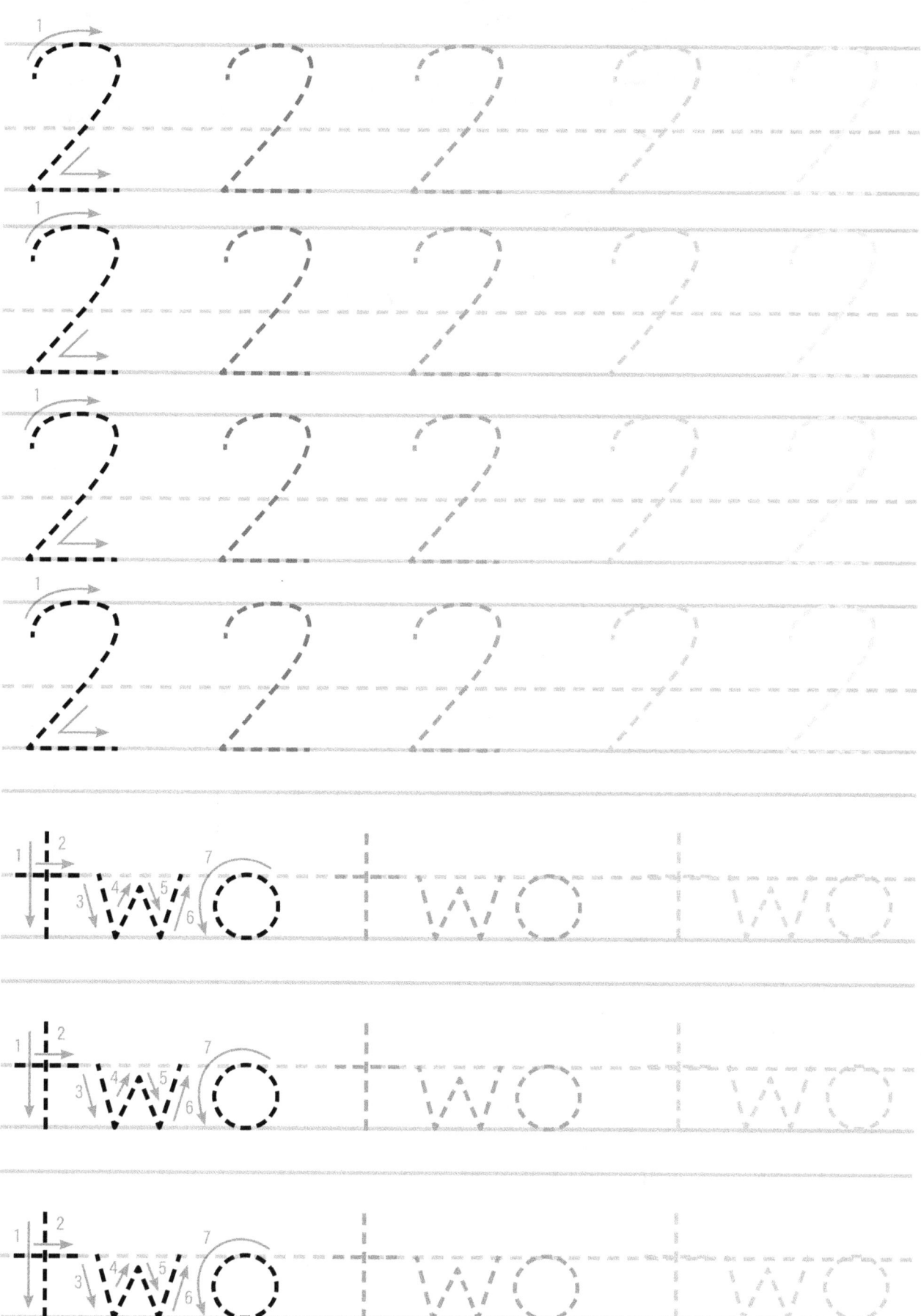

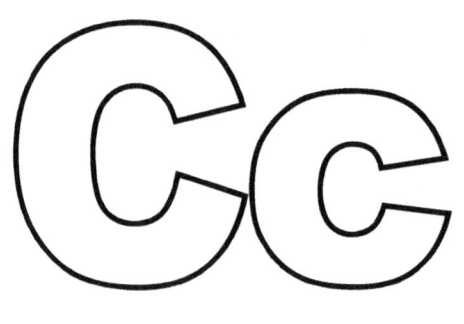 

C is for cake.
Trace the uppercase C and lowercase c. Color the letters and the pictures.

C is for cans.
Count the cans below. How many do you count? Write the number here:

Can you say the number 3 out loud?

Practice writing the number 3 and three.

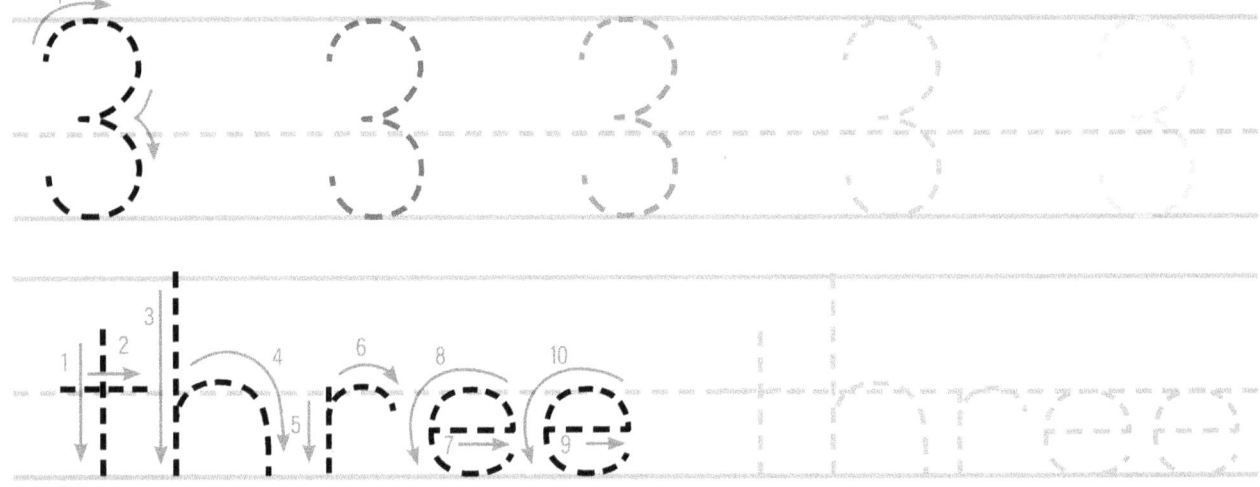

Practice writing the number 3 and three.

Dd

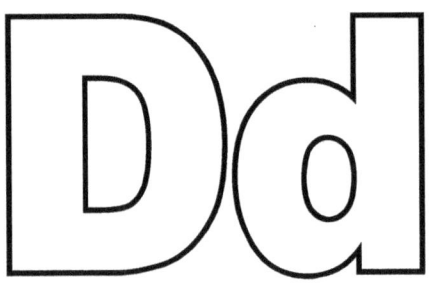

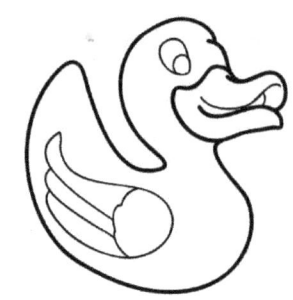

D is for duck.
Trace the uppercase D and lowercase d. Color the letters and the pictures.

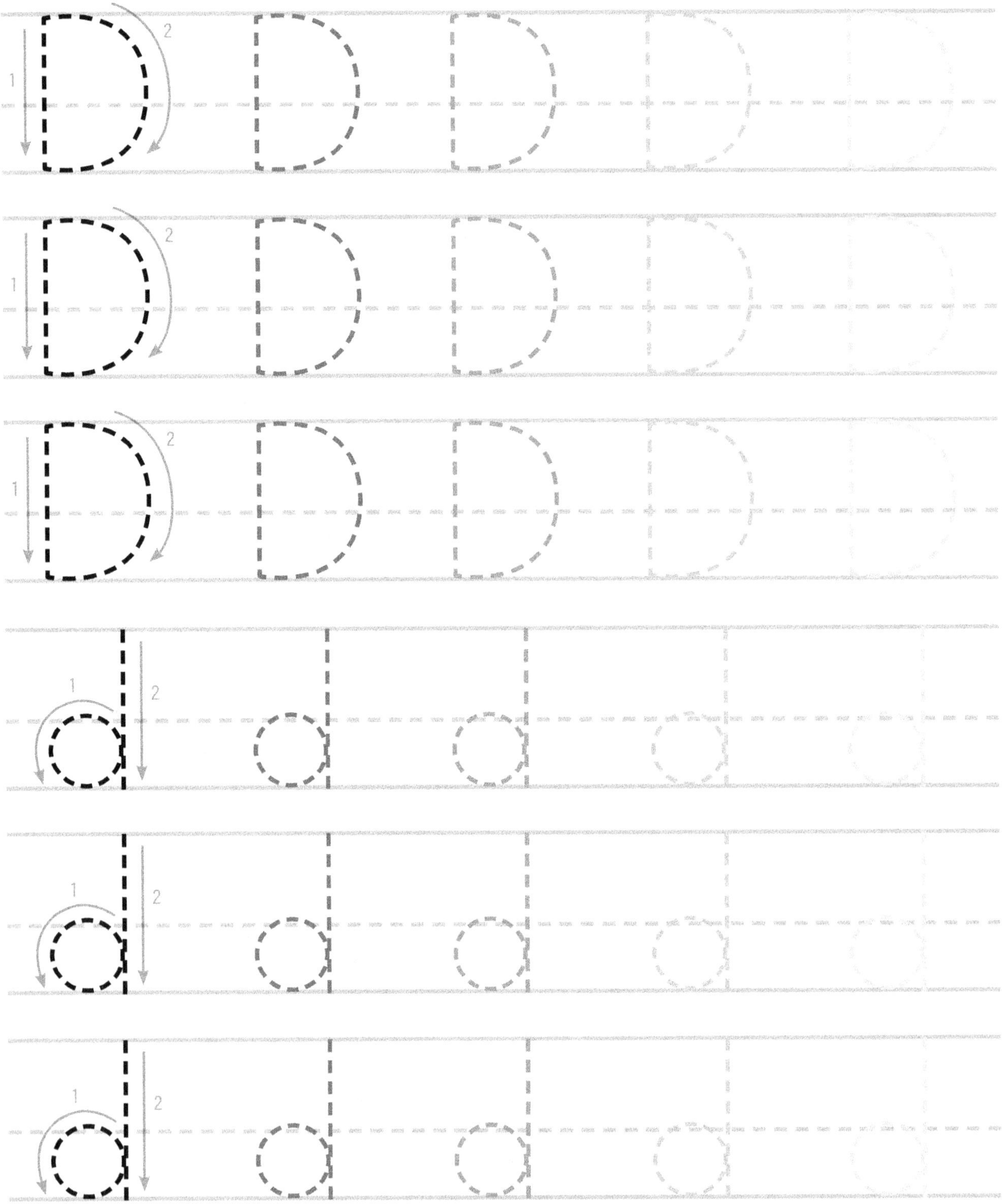

D is for dogs.
Count the dogs below. How many do you count? Write the number here:

Can you say the number 4 out loud?

Practice writing the number 4 and four.

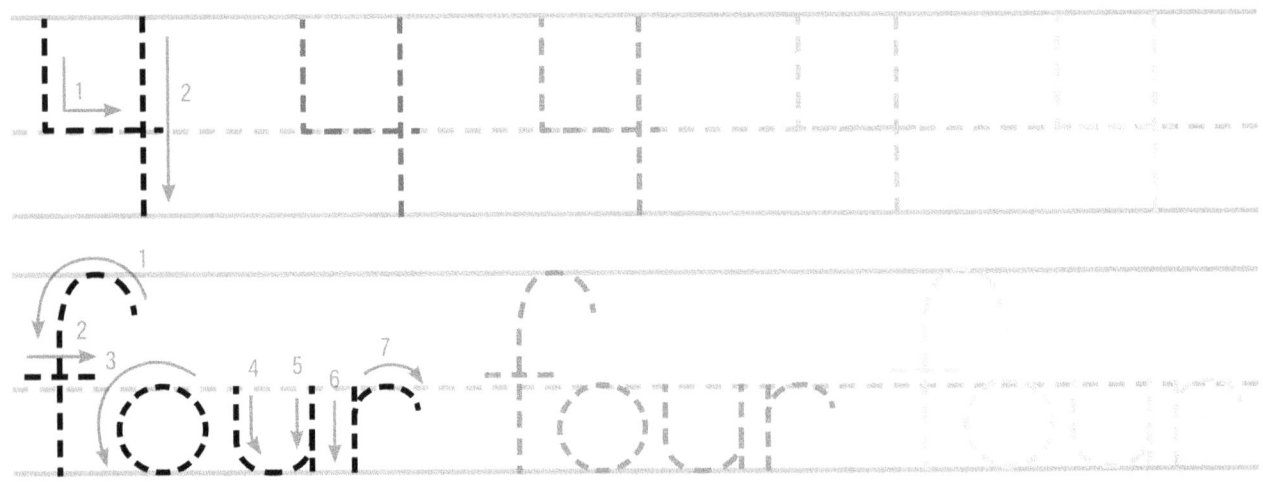

Practice writing the number 4 and four.

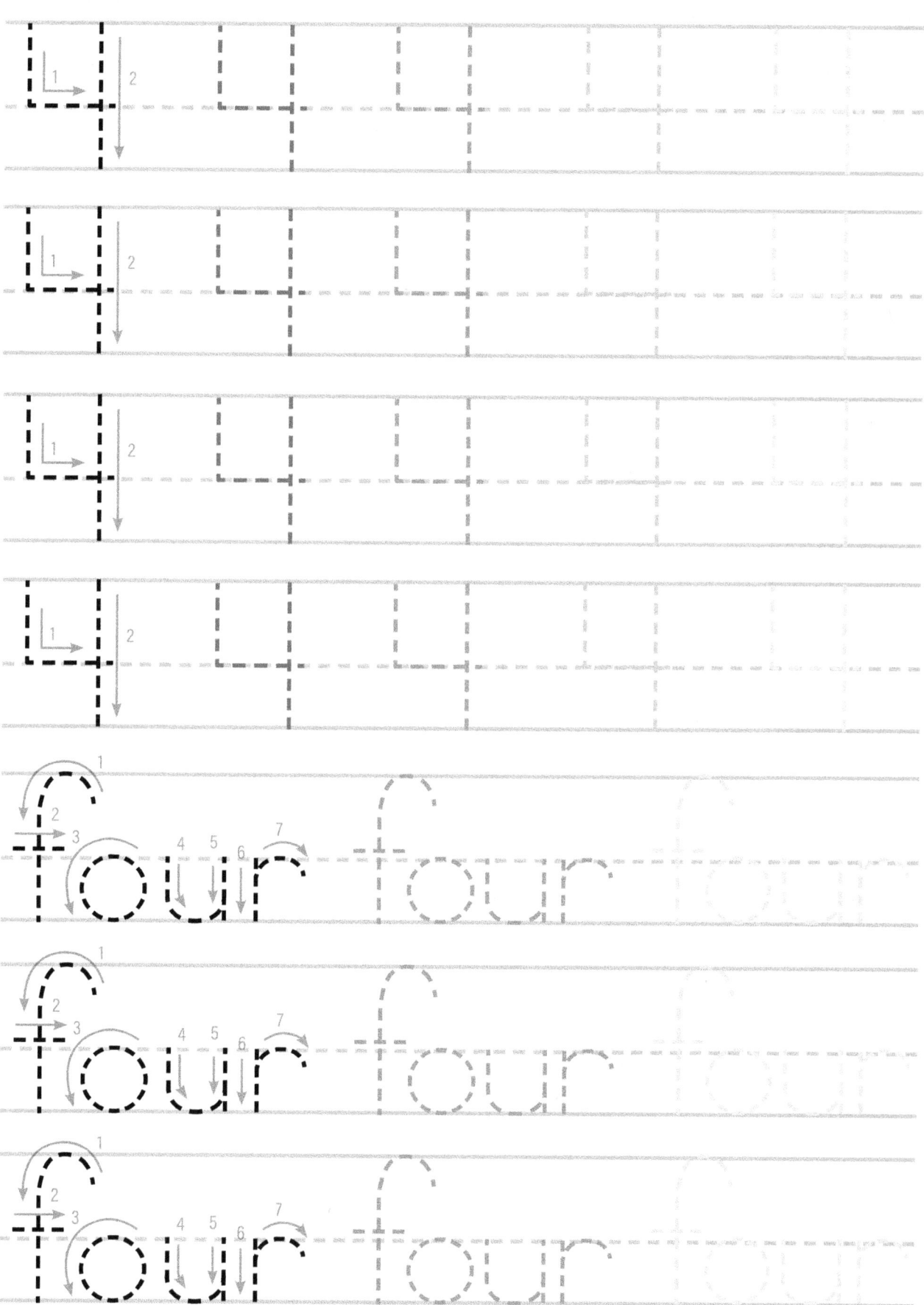

Ee

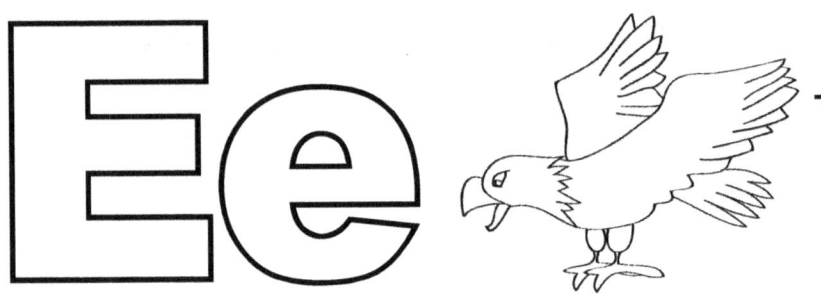

E is for eagle.
Trace the uppercase E and lowercase e. Color the letters and the pictures.

E is for eggs.
Count the eggs below. How many do you count? Write the number here:

Can you say the number 5 out loud?

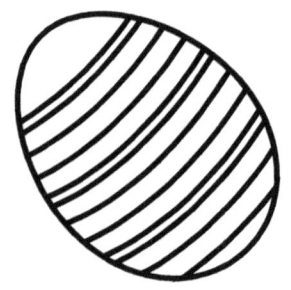

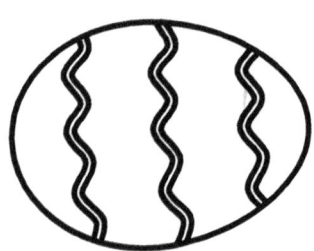

Practice writing the number 5 and five.

Practice writing the number 5 and five.

Ff

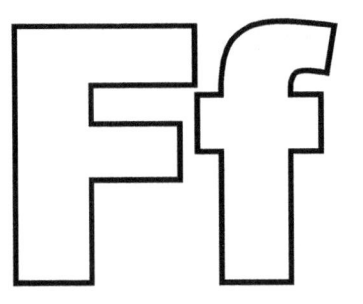

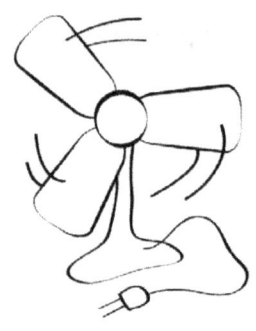

F is for fan.
Trace the uppercase F and lowercase f.
Color the letters and the pictures.

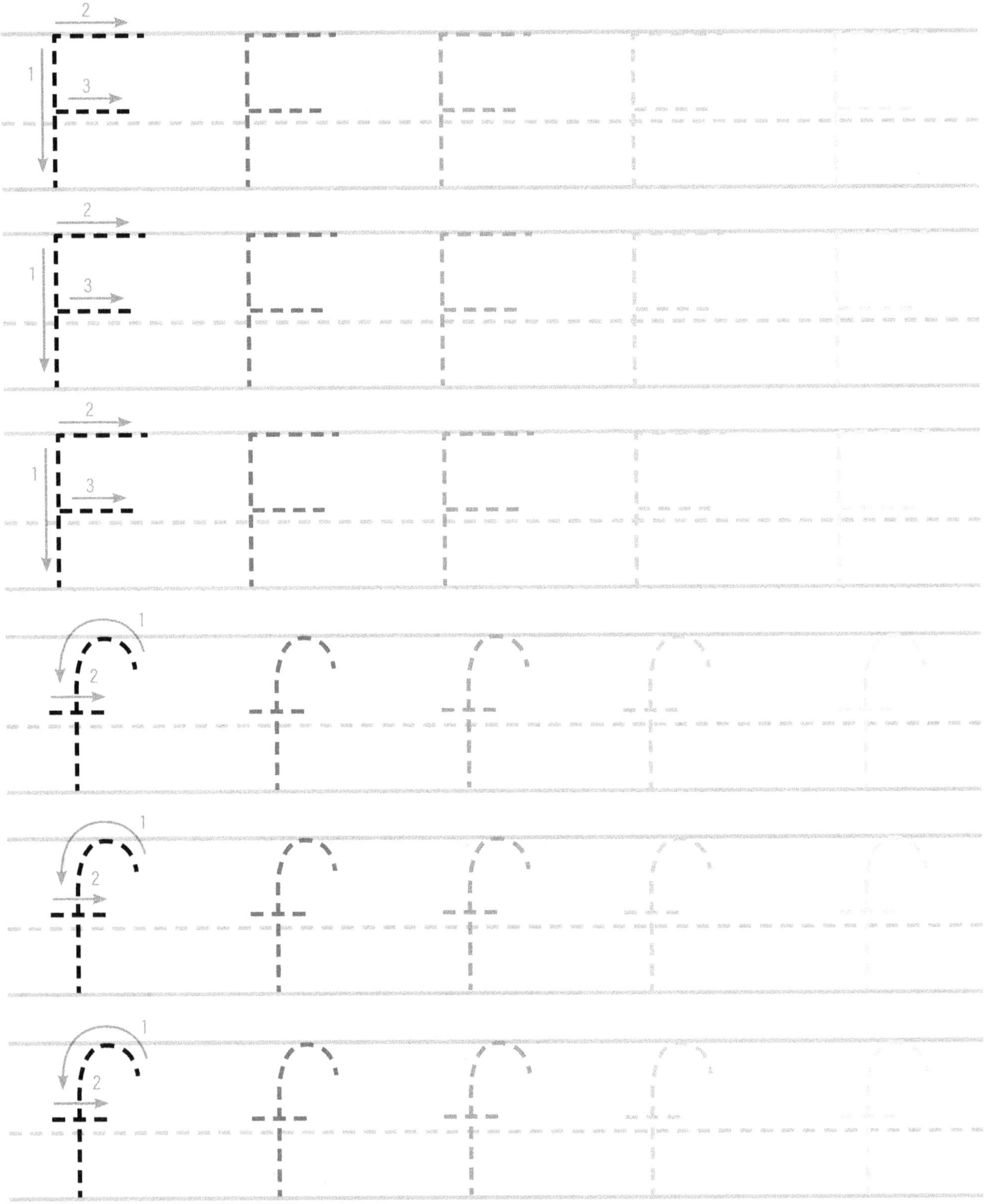

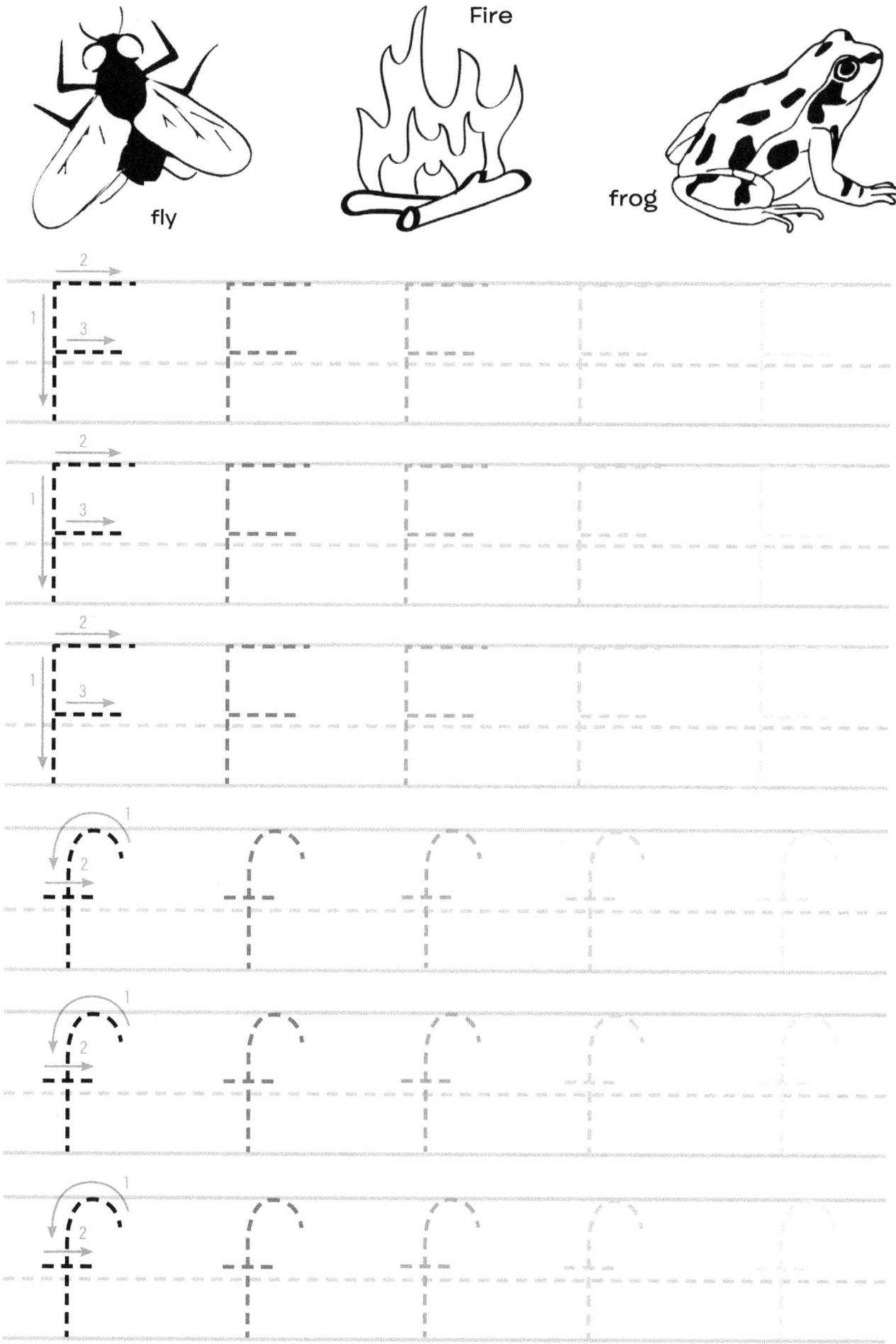

Six
6

F is for flags.
Count the flags below. How many do you count? Write the number here:

☐

Can you say the number 6 out loud?

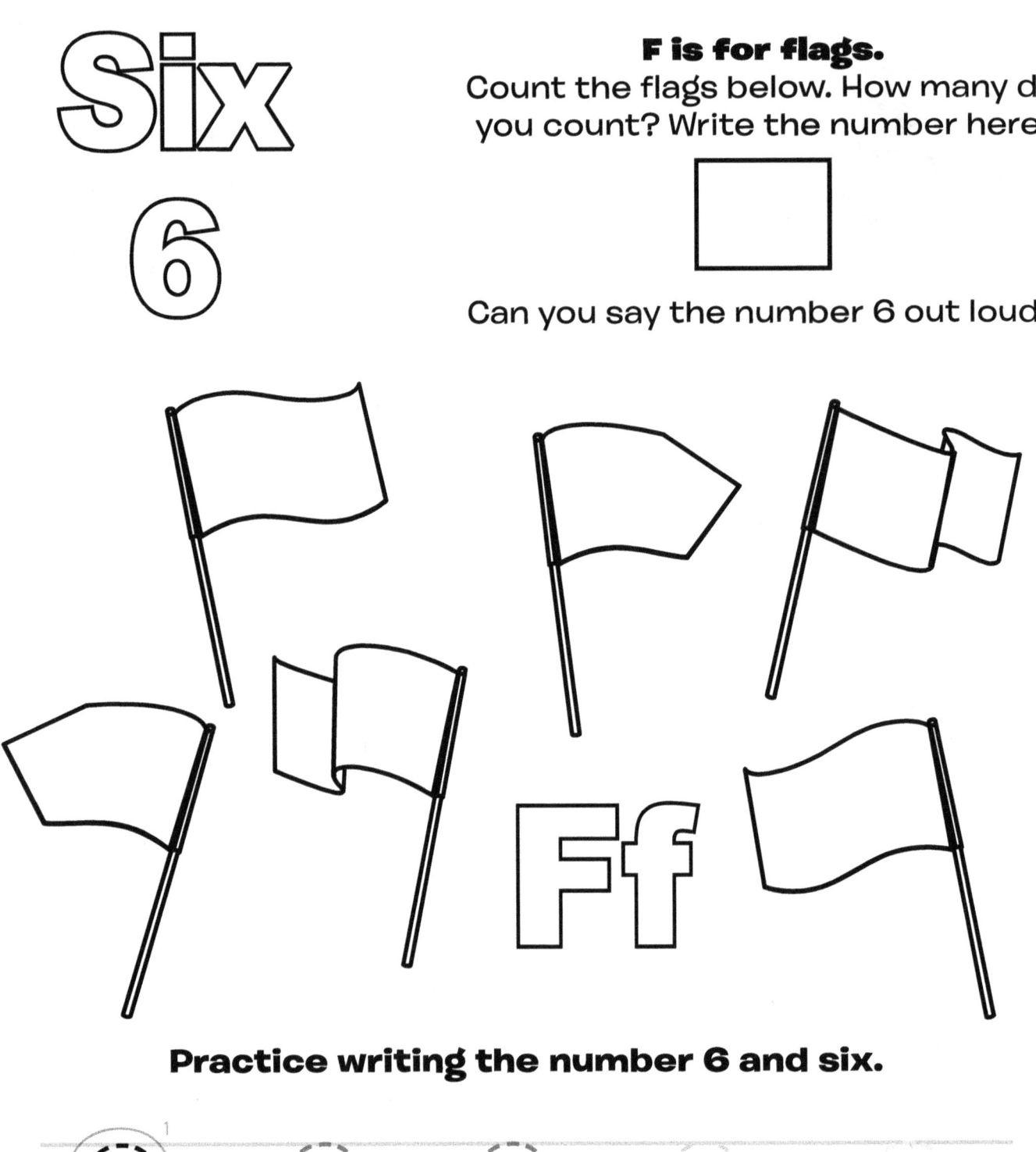

Practice writing the number 6 and six.

Practice writing the number 6 and six.

Seven
7

G is for gift.
Count the gifts below. How many do you count? Write the number here:

☐

Can you say the number 7 out loud?

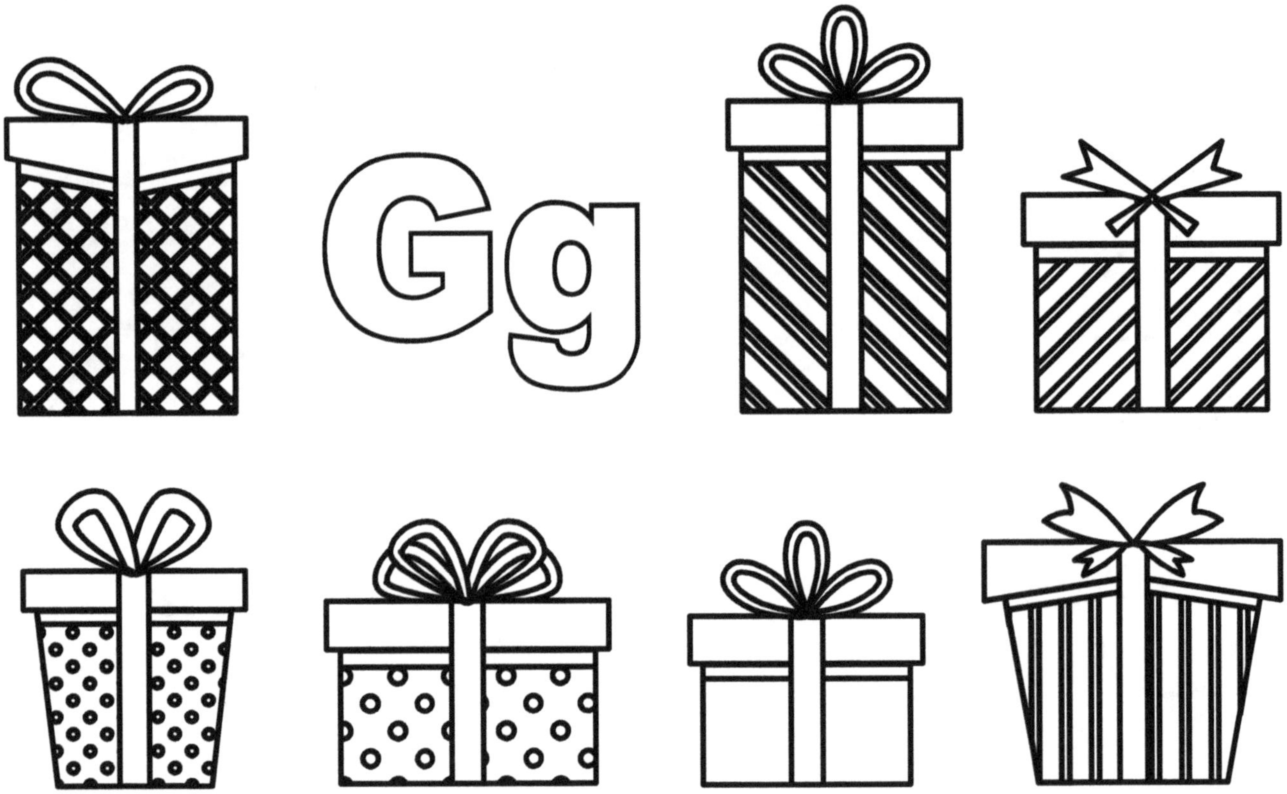

Practice writing the number 7 and seven.

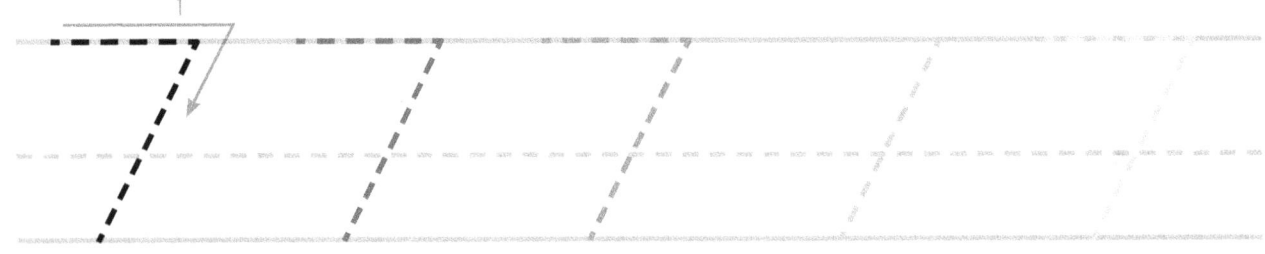

Practice writing the number 7 and seven.

Hh

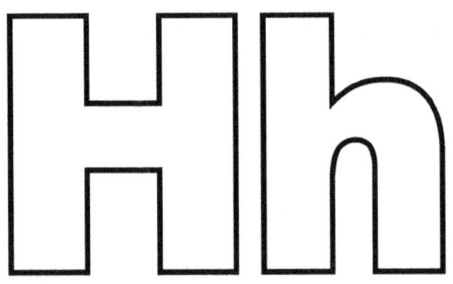

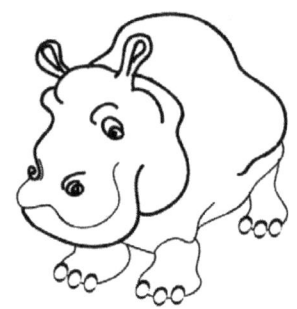

H is for hippo.
Trace the uppercase H and lowercase h. Color the letters and the pictures.

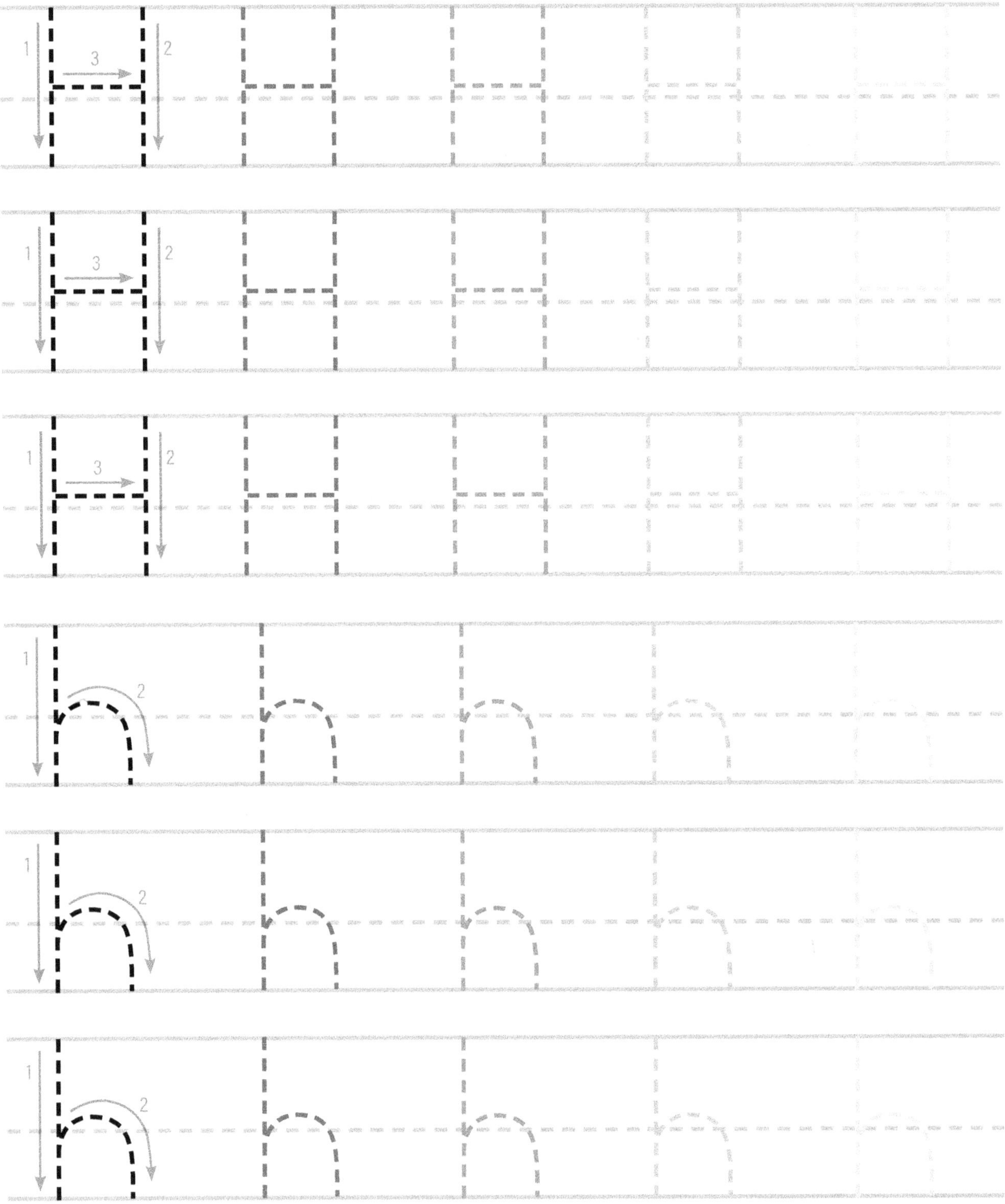

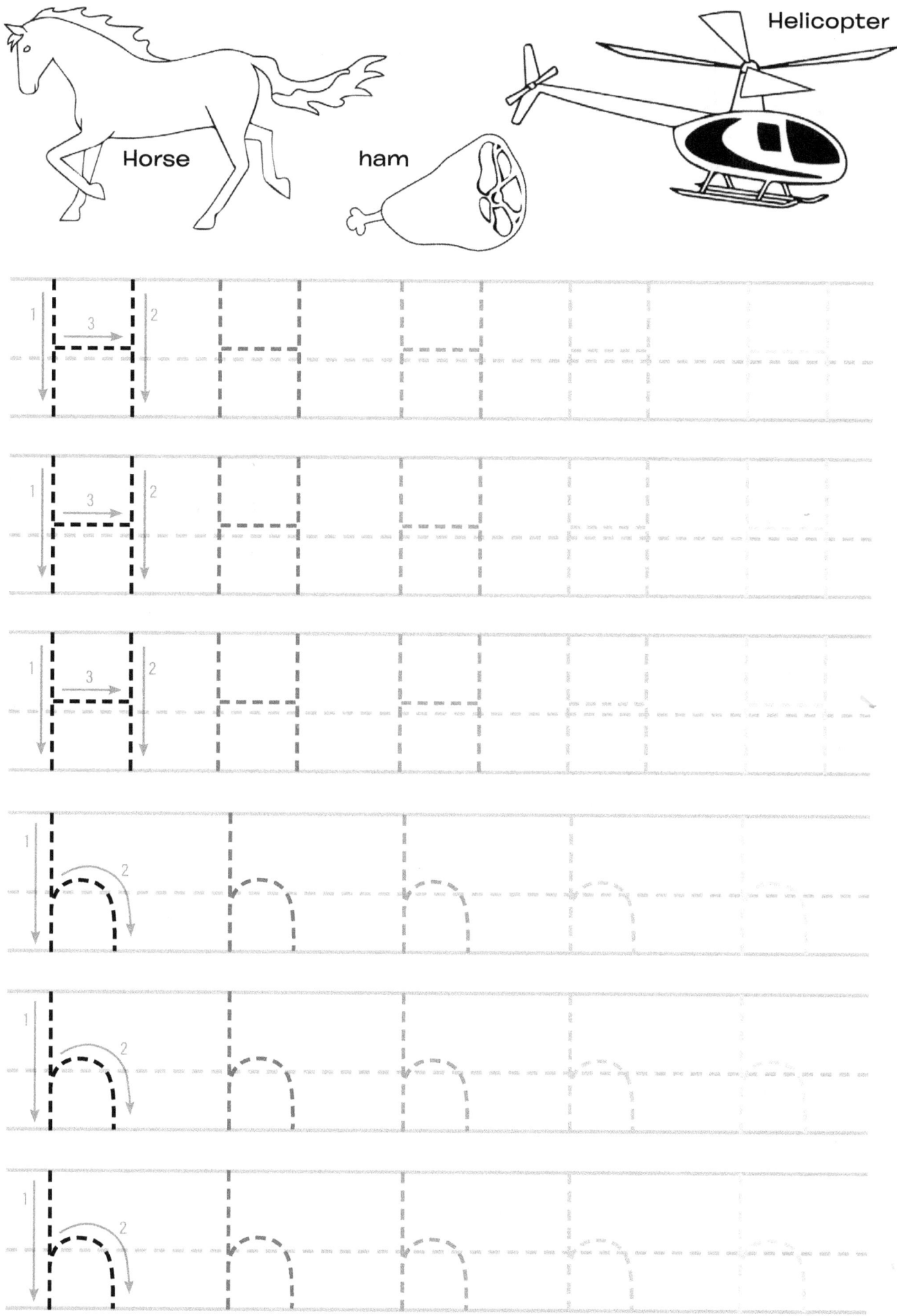

H is for house.
Count the houses below. How many do you count? Write the number here:

Can you say the number 8 out loud?

Practice writing the number 8 and eight.

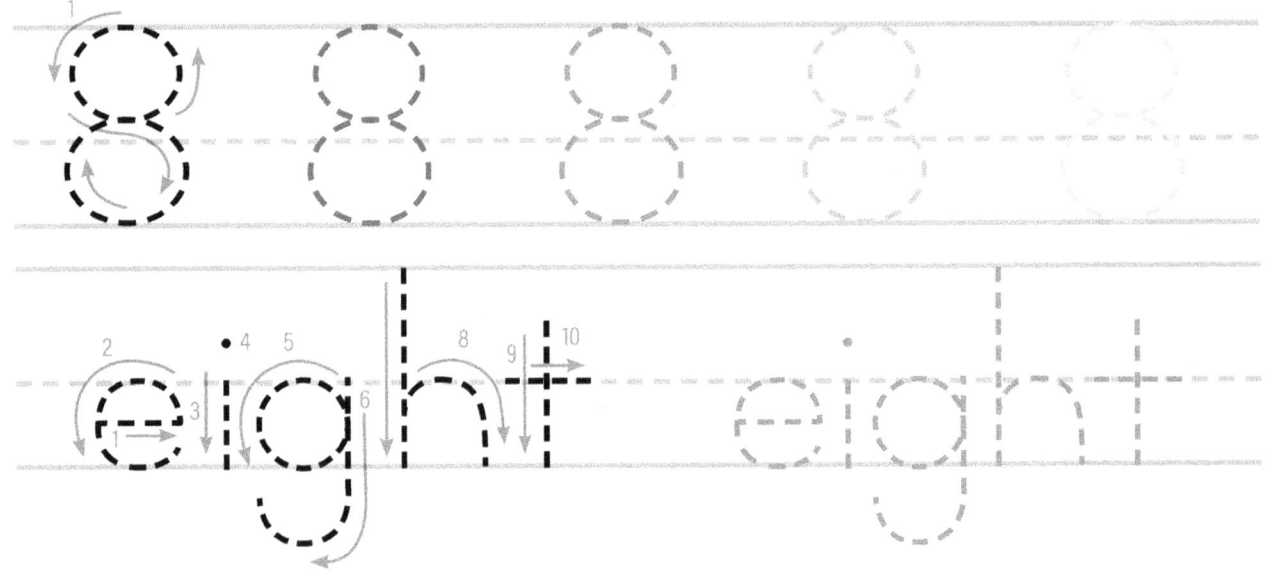

Practice writing the number 8 and eight.

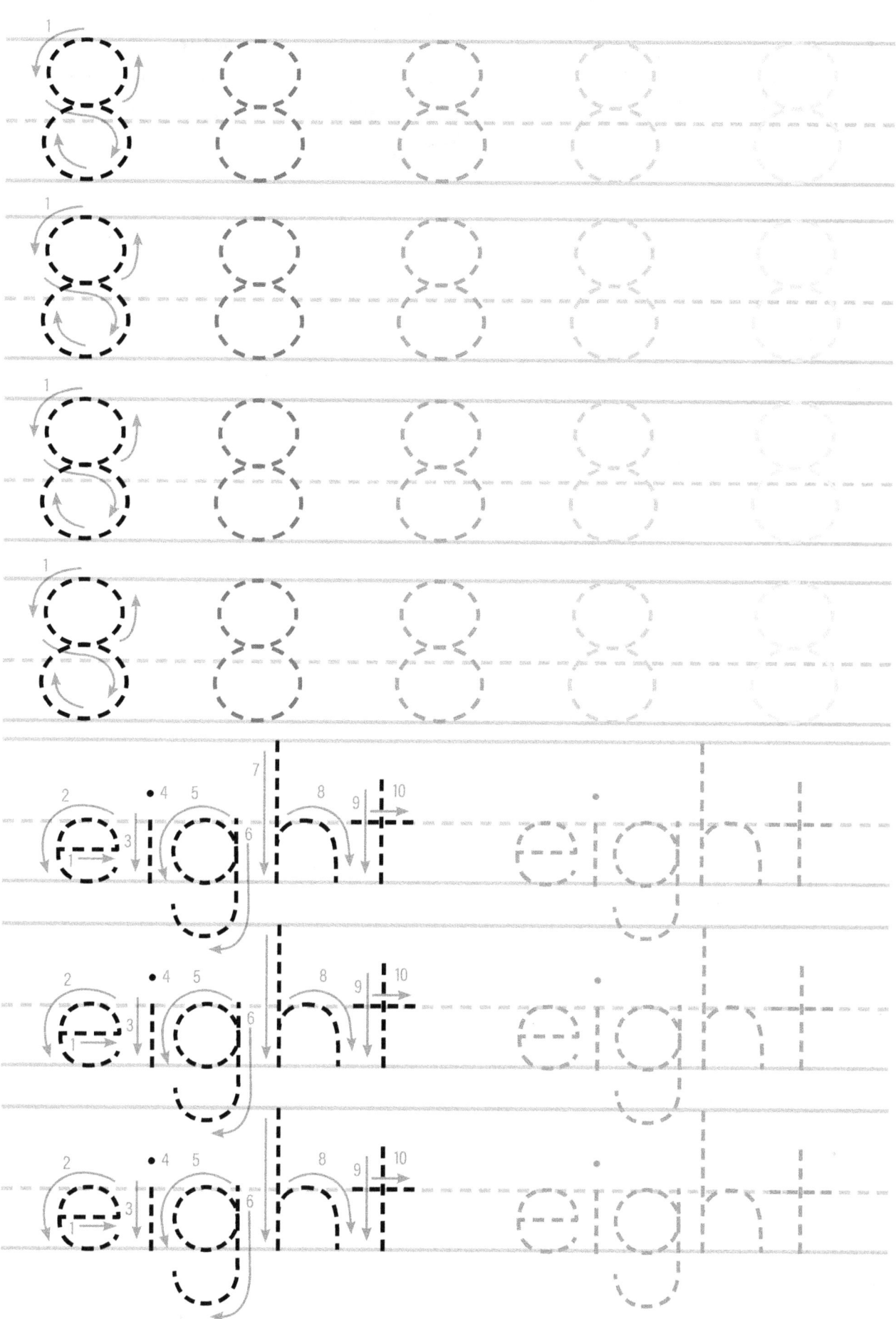

I i

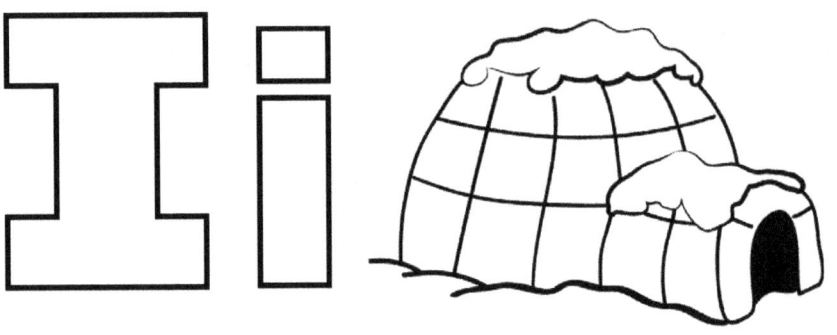

I is for igloo.
Trace the uppercase I and lowercase i. Color the letters and the pictures.

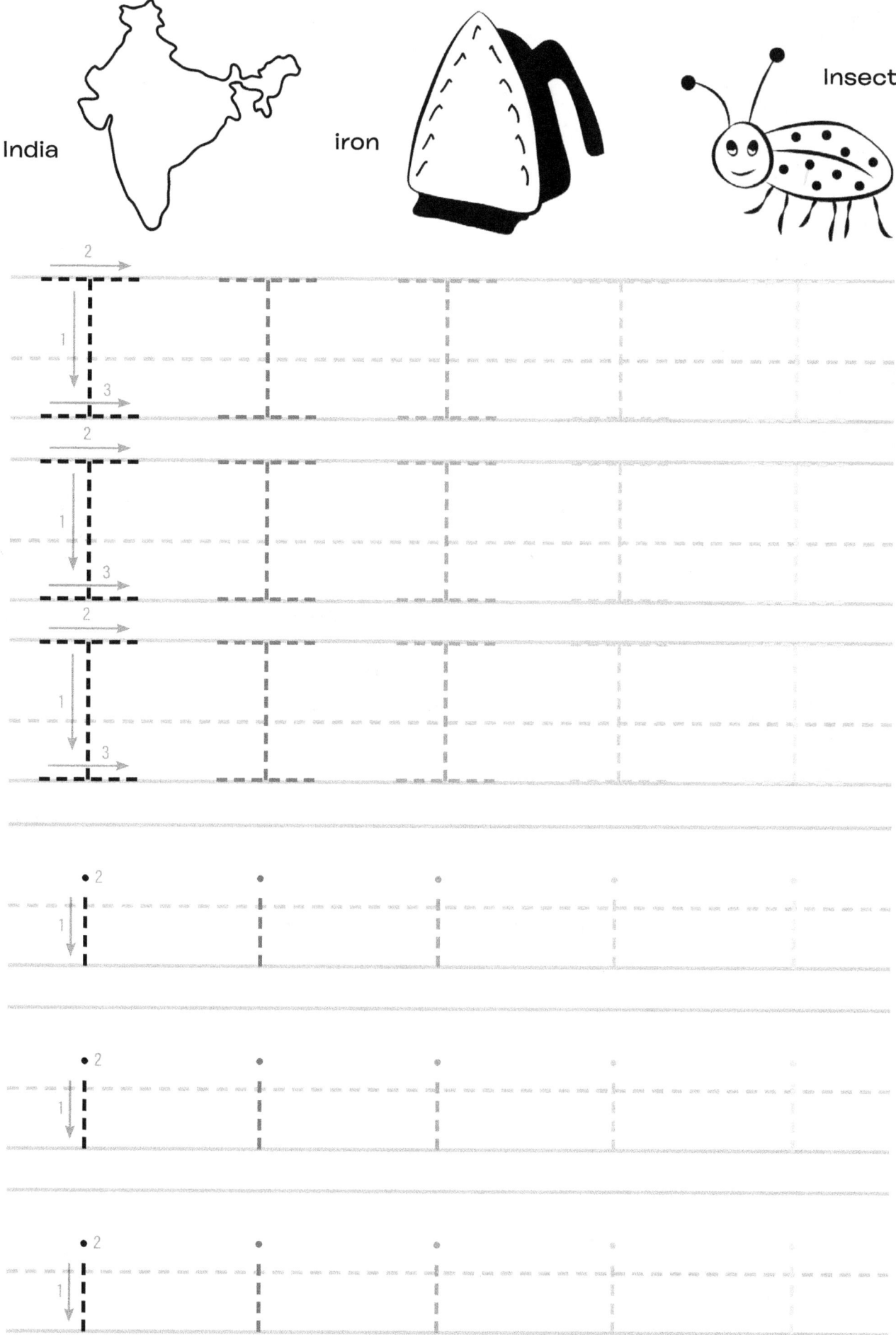

India   iron   Insect

I is for ice.
Count the ice cubes below. How many do you count? Write the number here:

Can you say the number 9 out loud?

Practice writing the number 9 and nine.

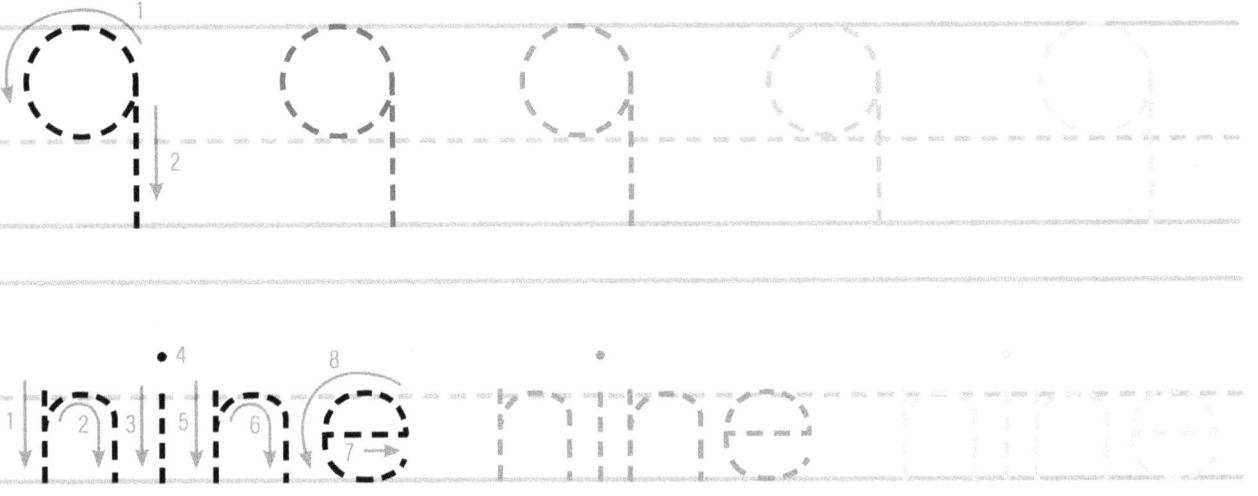

Practice writing the number 9 and nine.

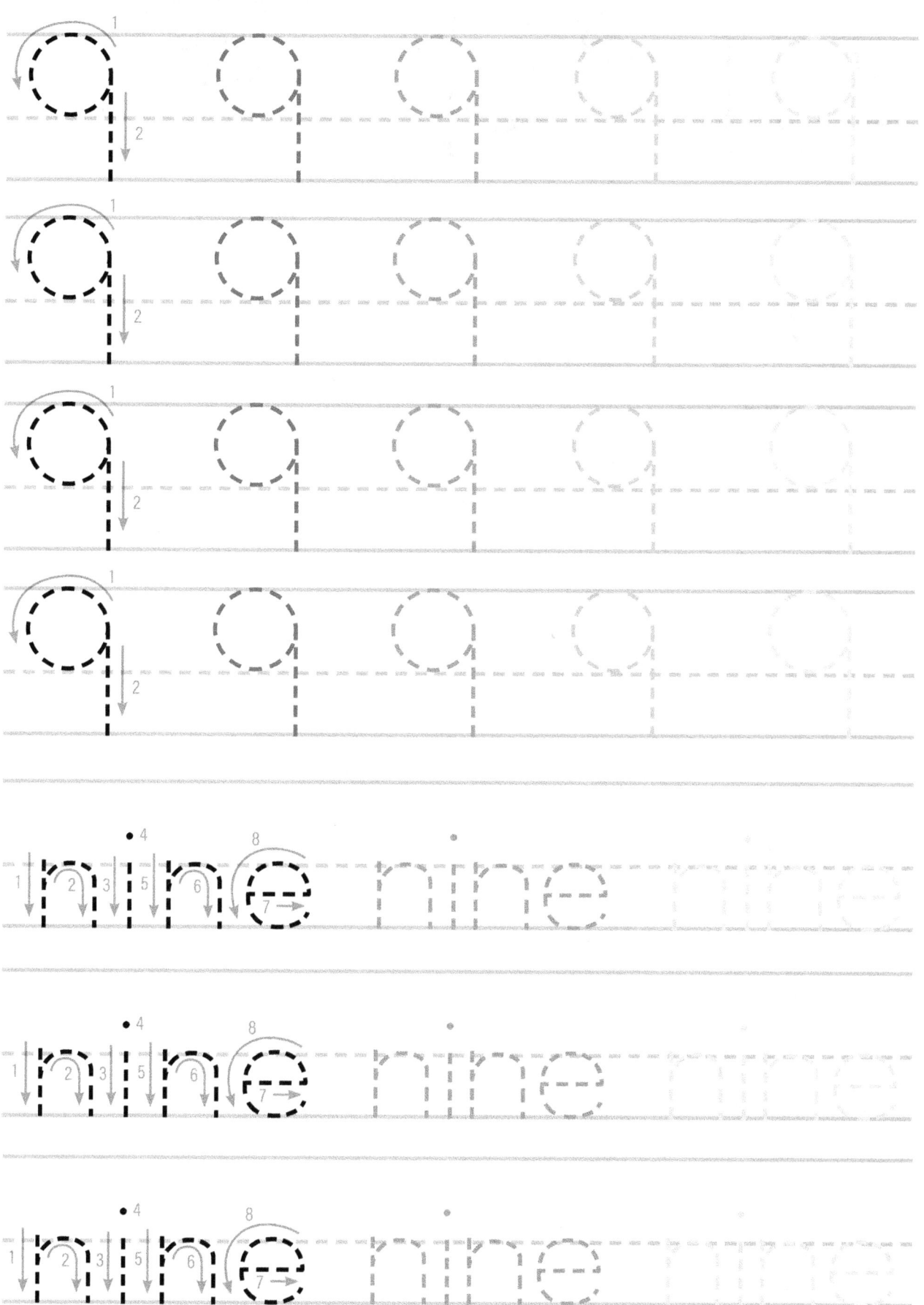

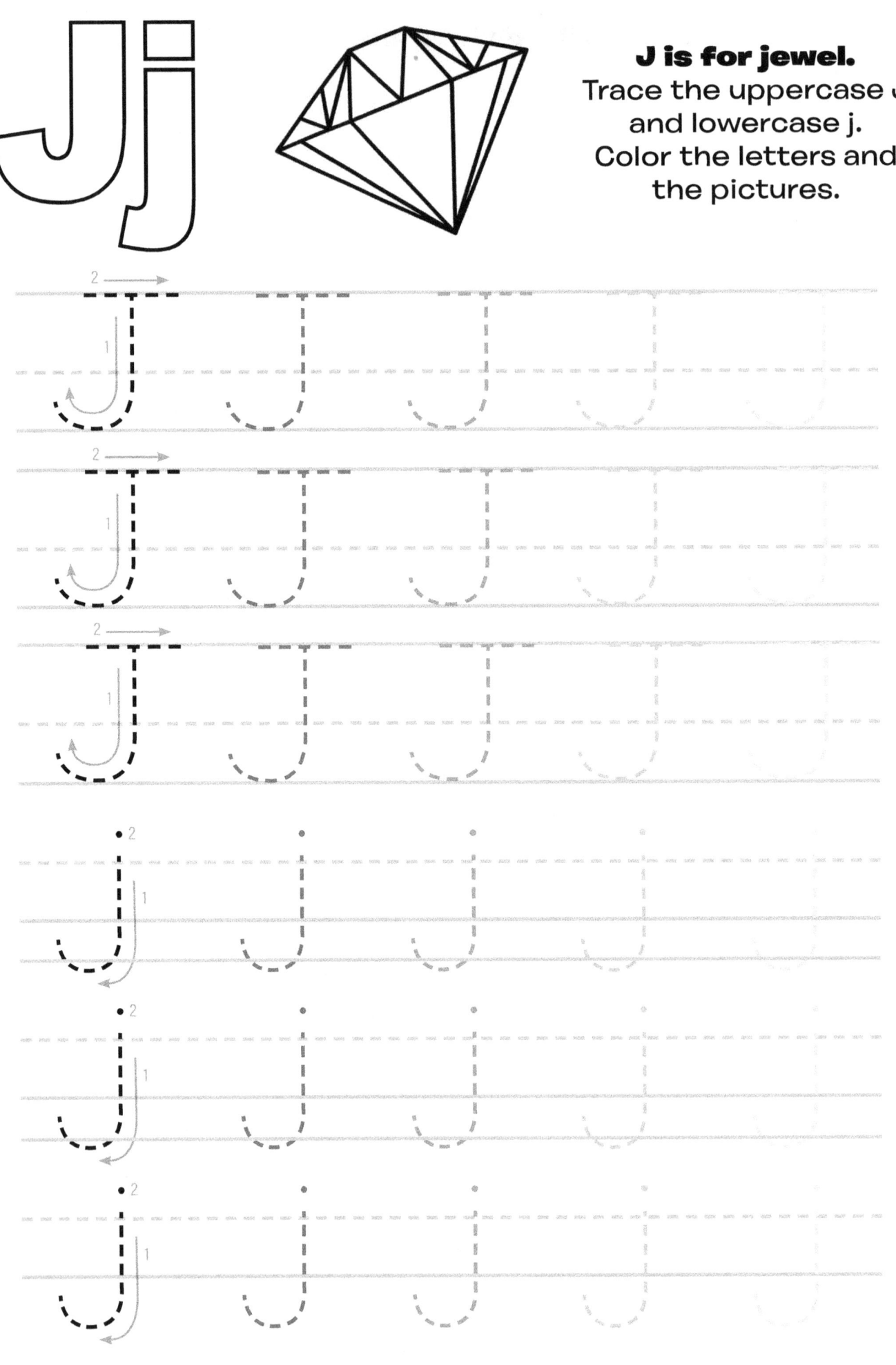

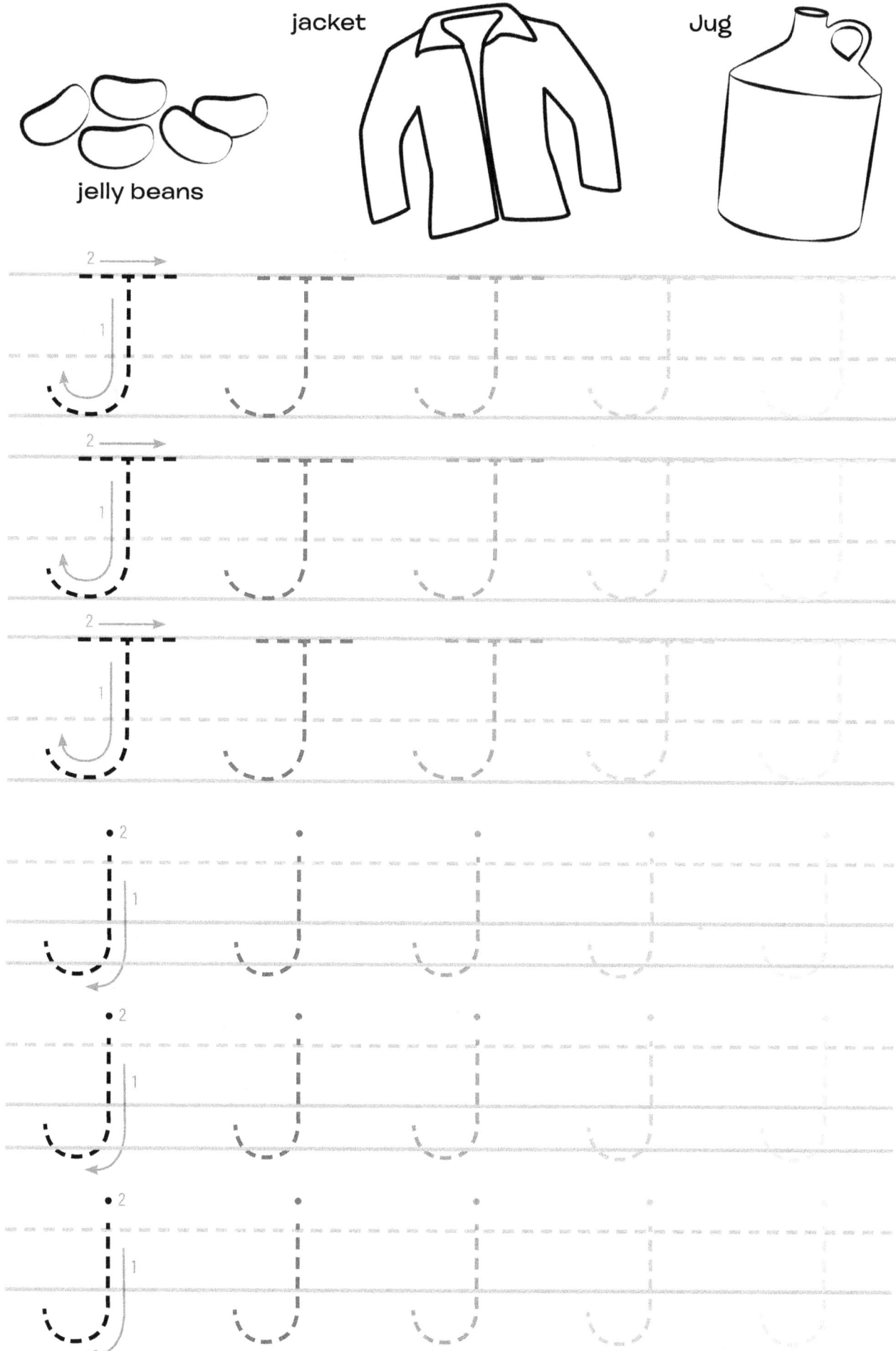

Ten
10

J is for jars.
Count the jars below. How many do you count? Write the number here:

☐

Can you say the number 10 out loud?

Practice writing the number 10 and ten.

Practice writing the number 10 and ten.

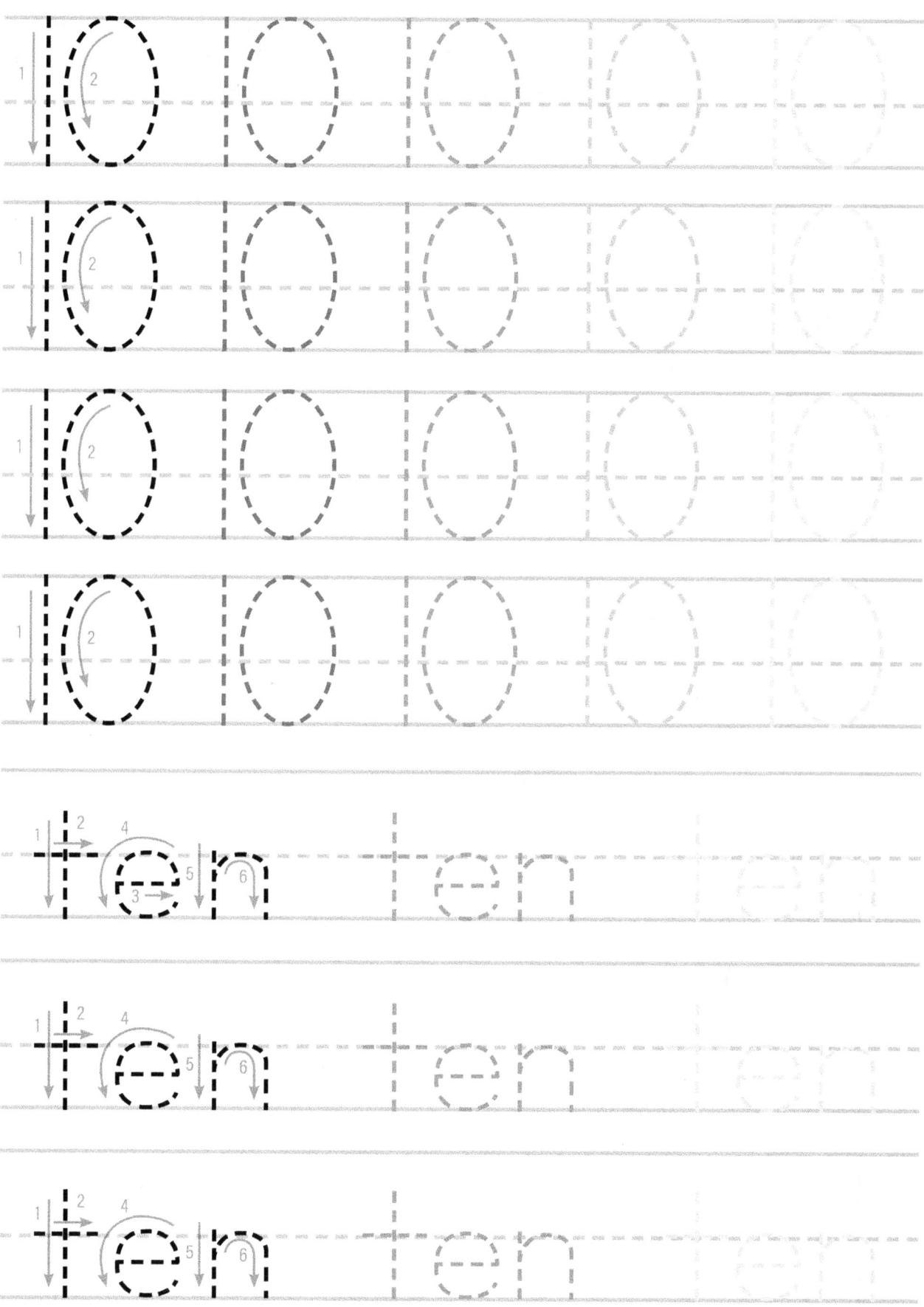

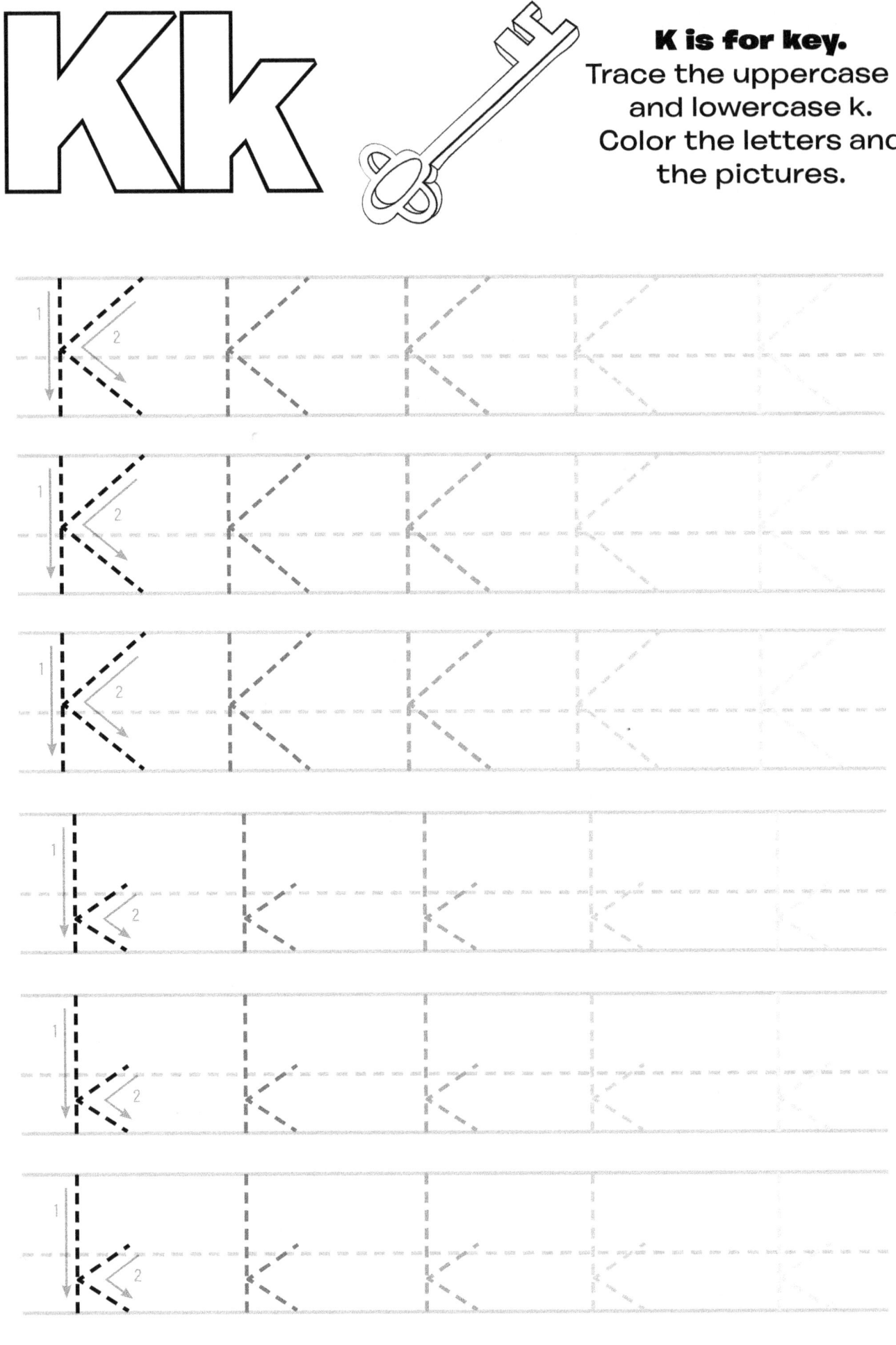

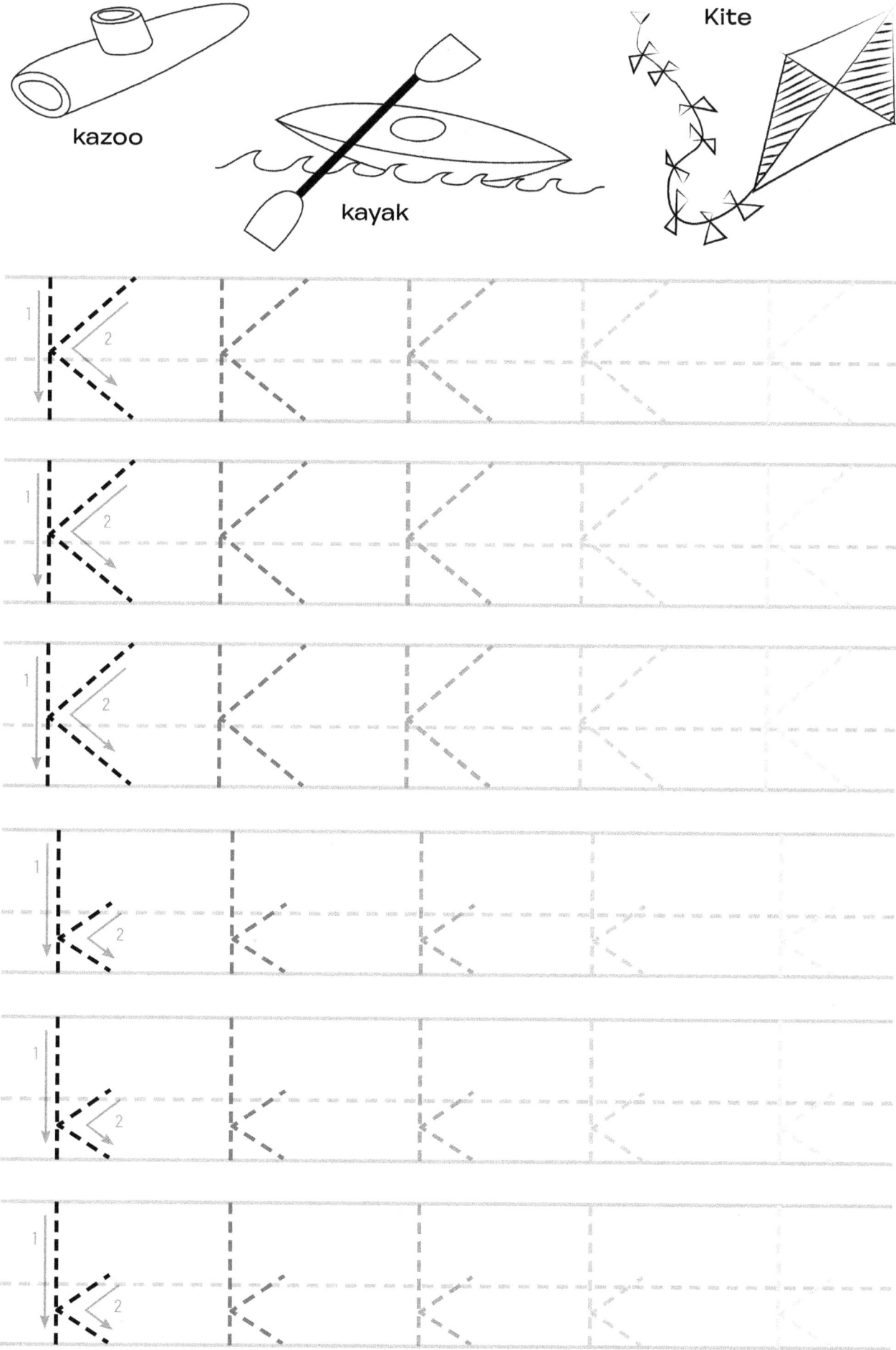

Ll

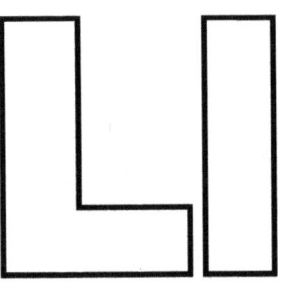

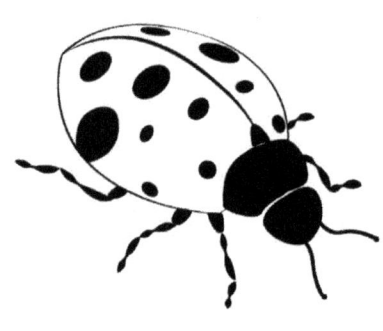

L is for ladybug.
Trace the uppercase L
and lowercase l.
Color the letters and
the pictures.

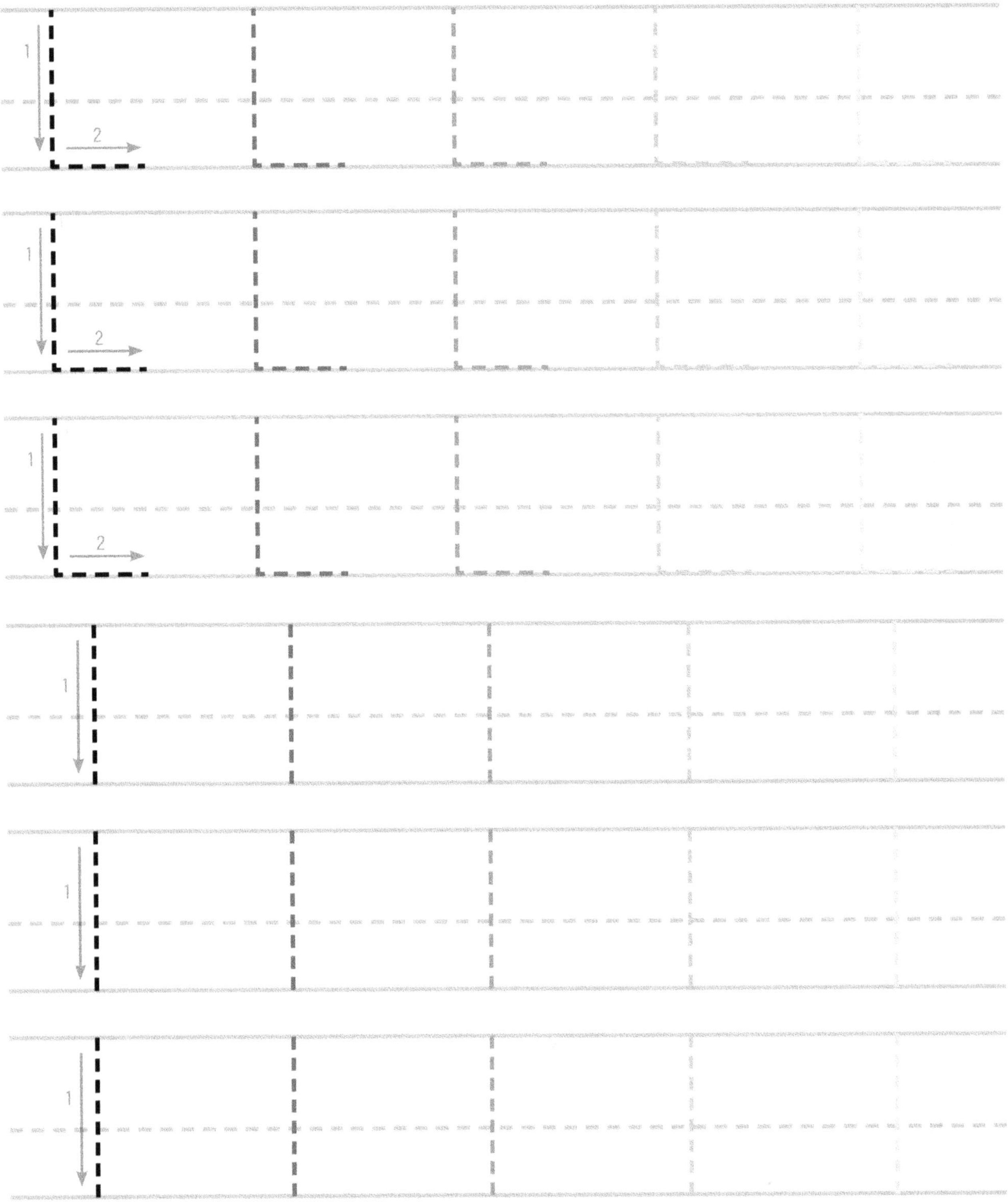

Mm

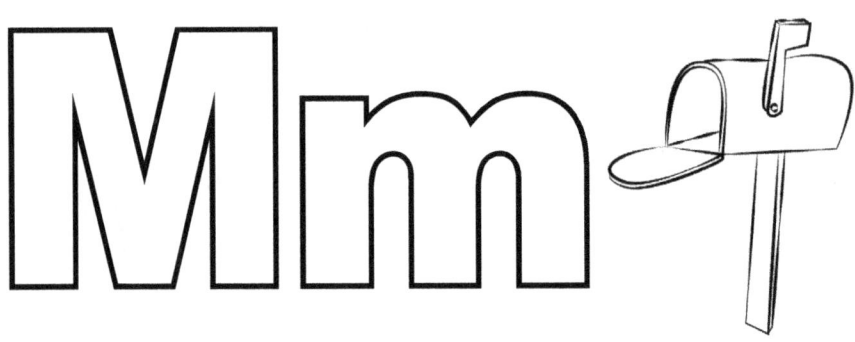

M is for mailbox.
Trace the uppercase M and lowercase m.
Color the letters and the pictures.

M M M M M

M M M M M

M M M M M

m m m m m

m m m m m

m m m m m

N is for net.
Trace the uppercase N and lowercase n. Color the letters and the pictures.

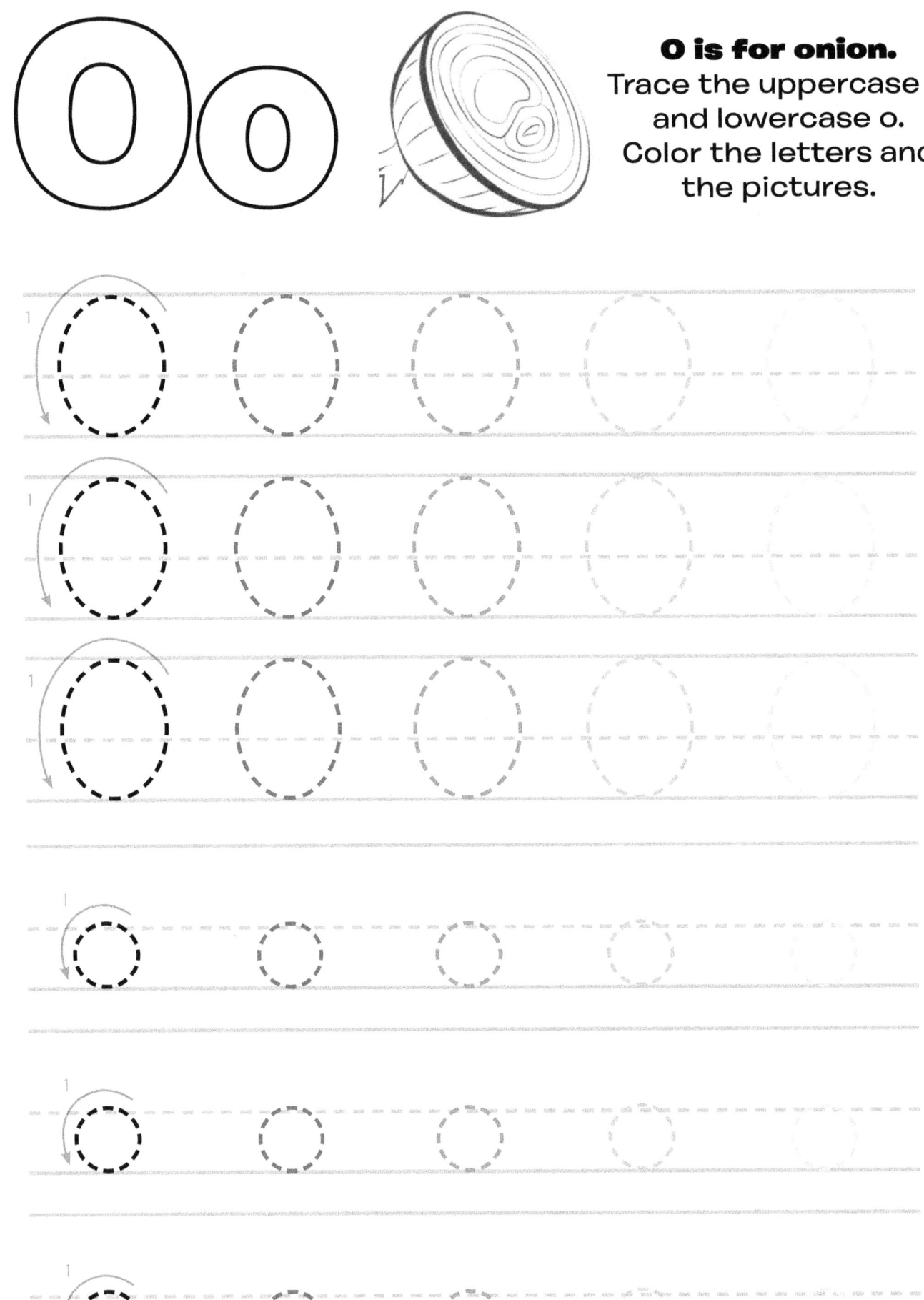

O is for onion.
Trace the uppercase O and lowercase o. Color the letters and the pictures.

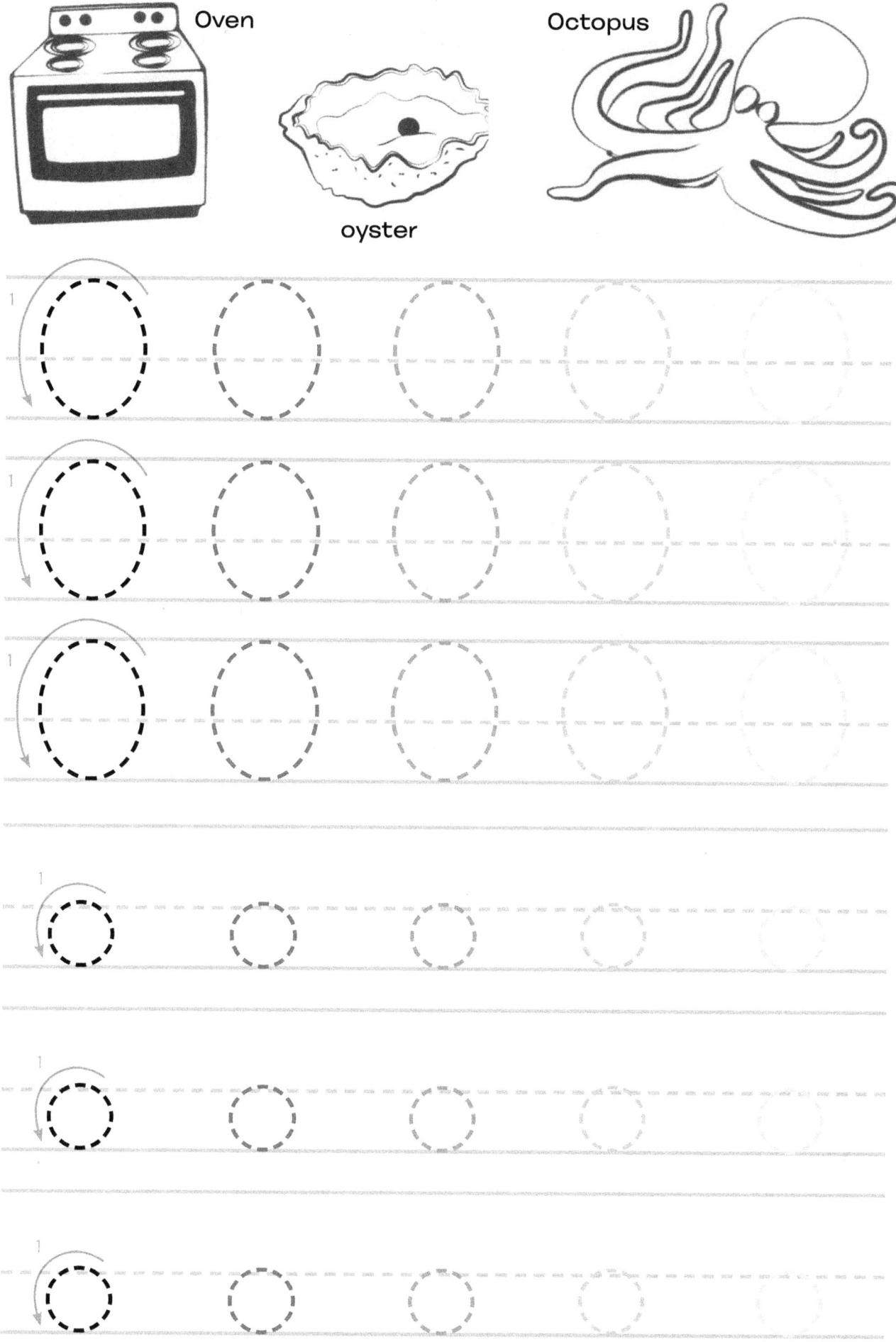

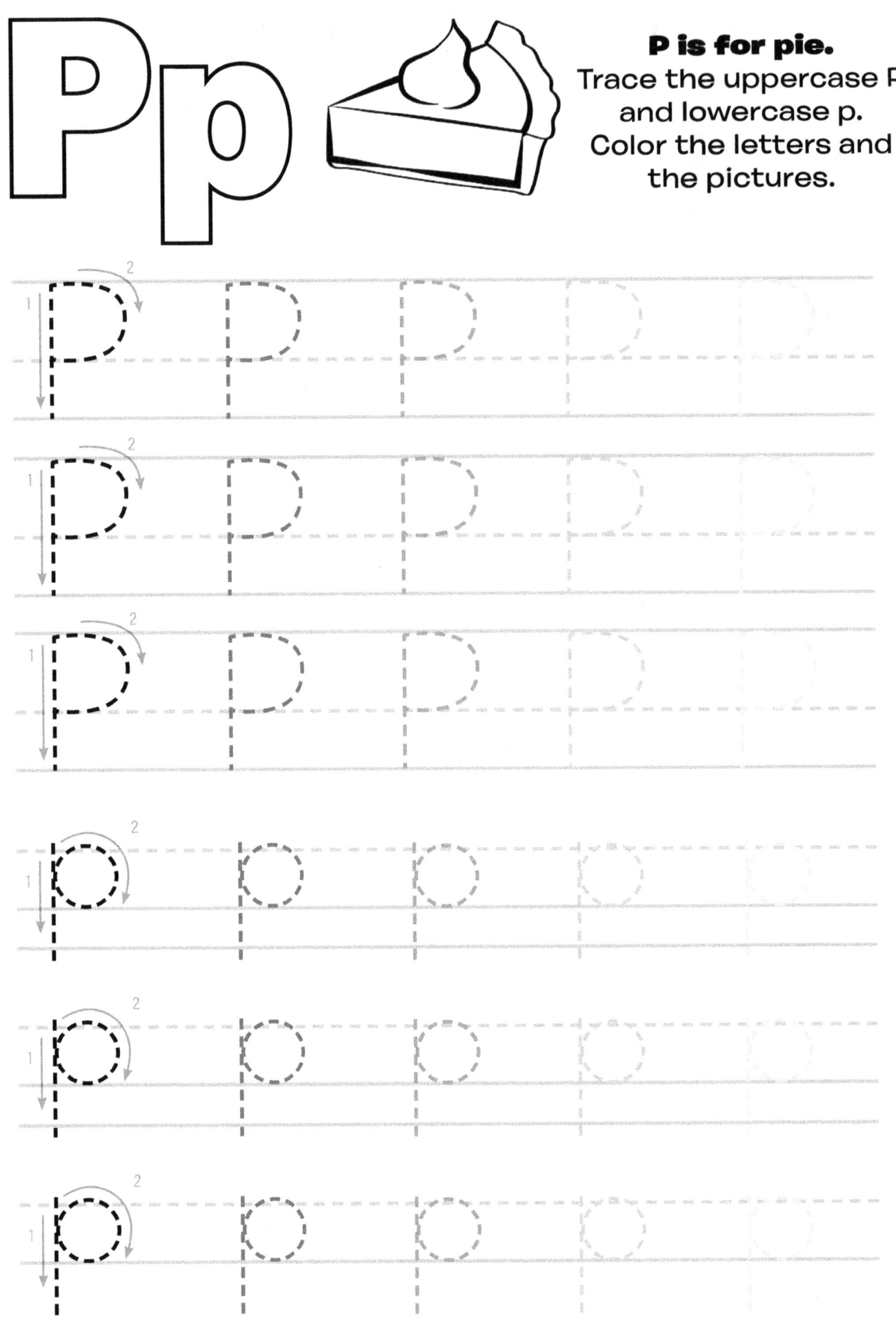

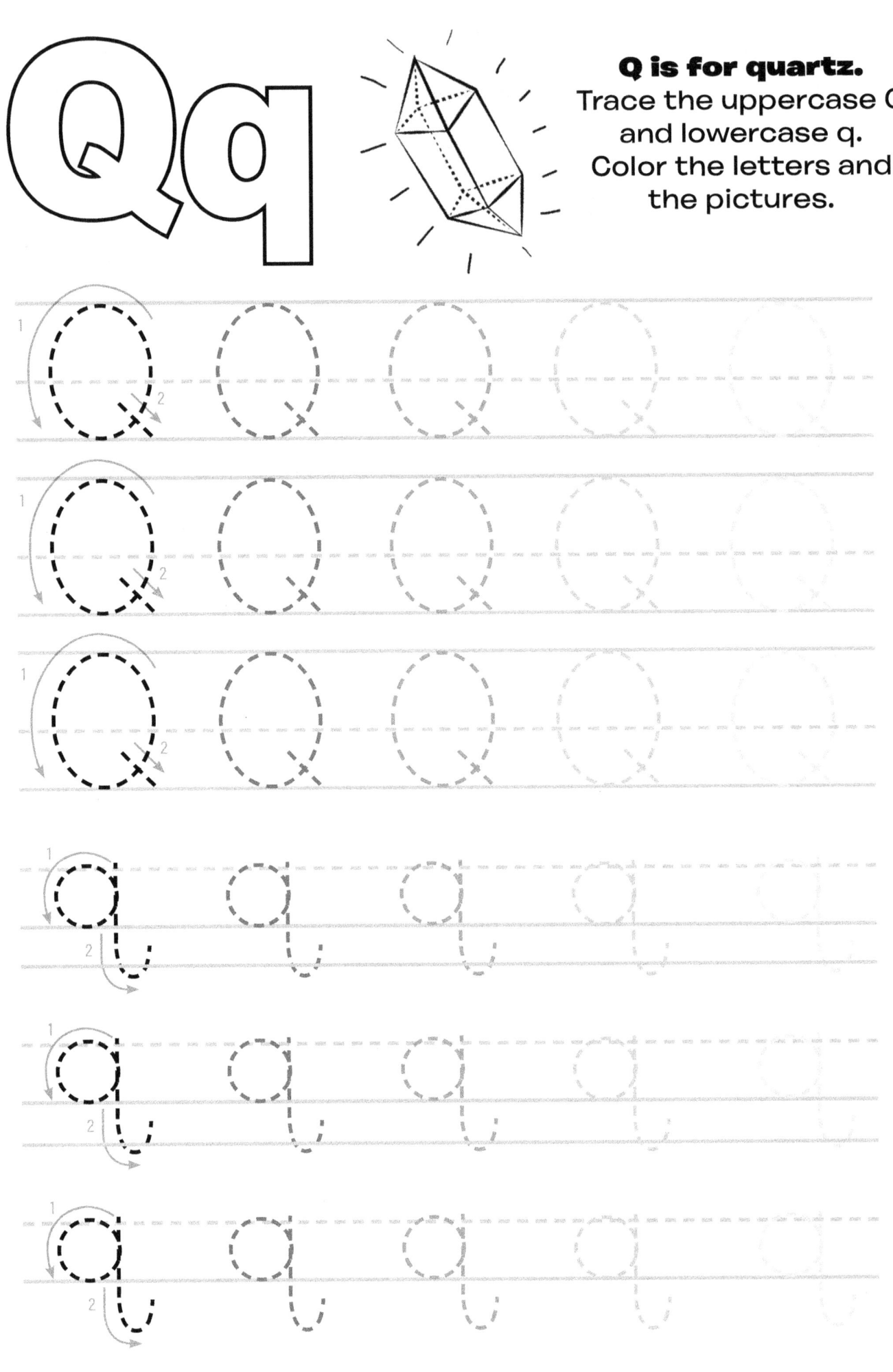

Q is for quartz.
Trace the uppercase Q and lowercase q. Color the letters and the pictures.

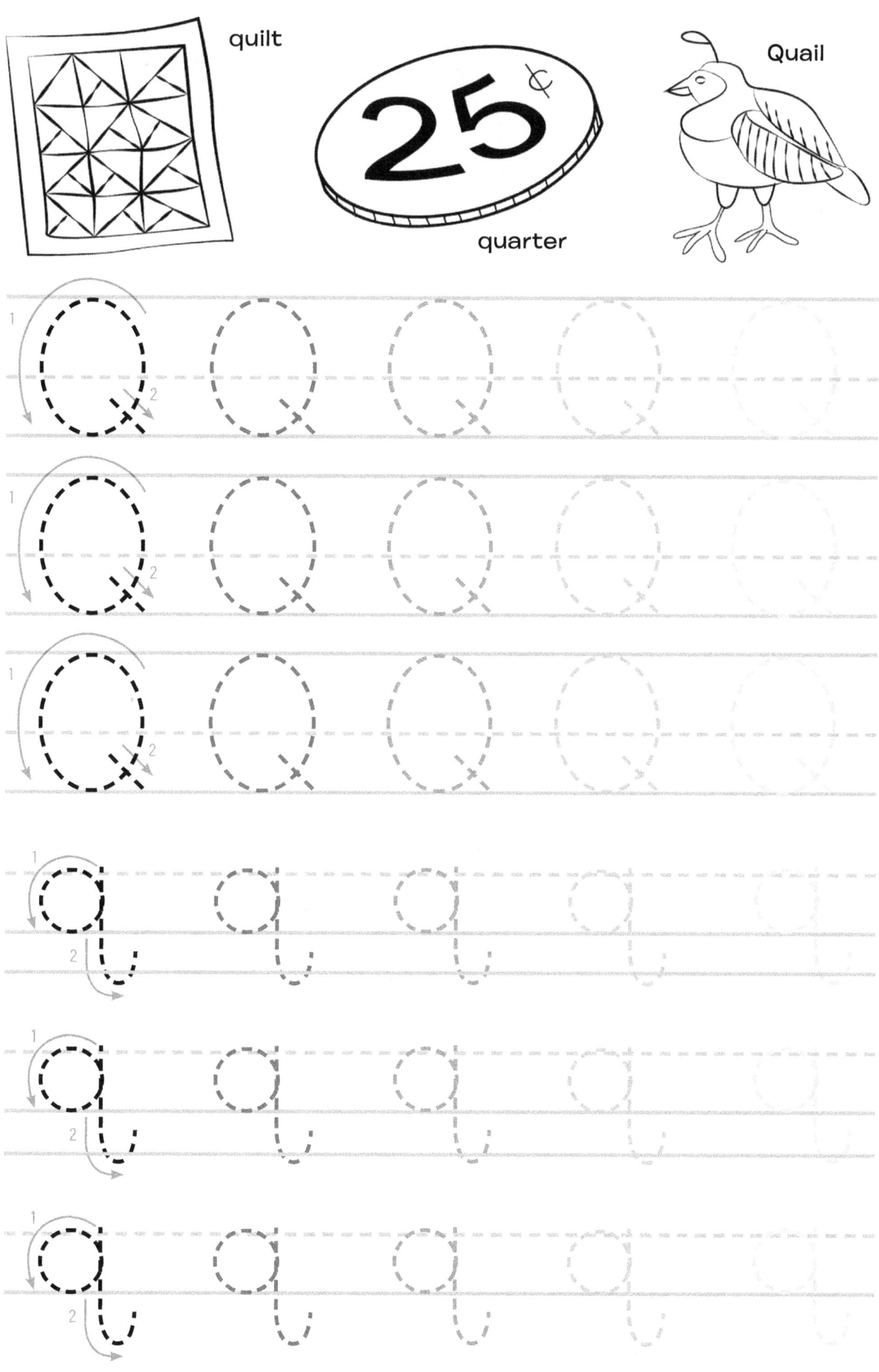

Rr

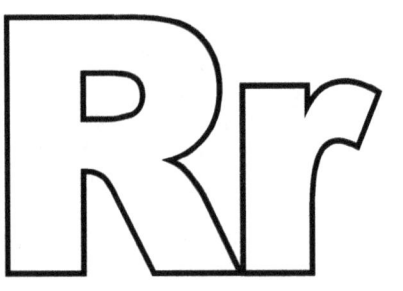

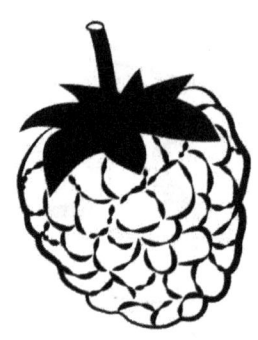

R is for raspberry.
Trace the uppercase R and lowercase r.
Color the letters and the pictures.

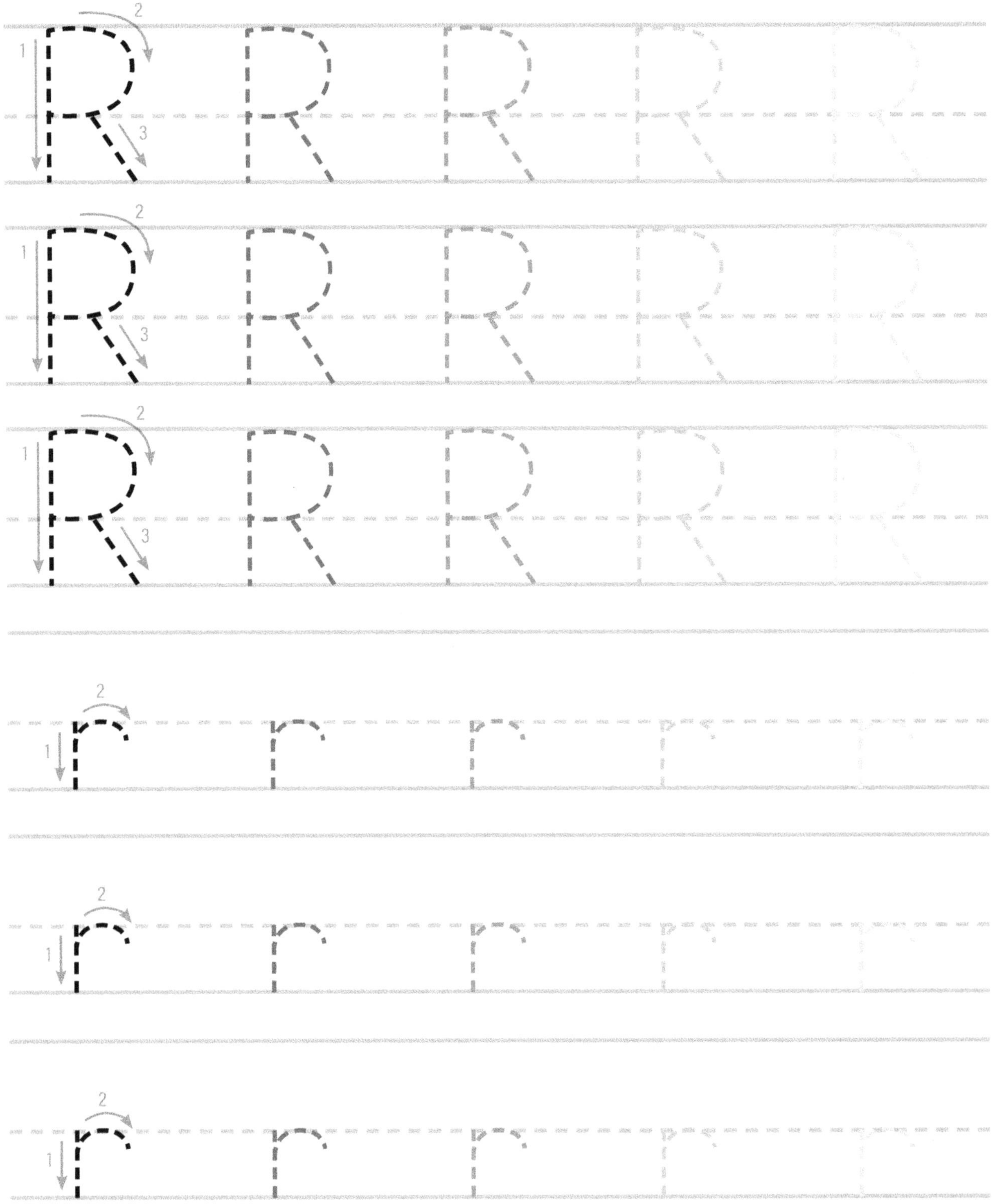

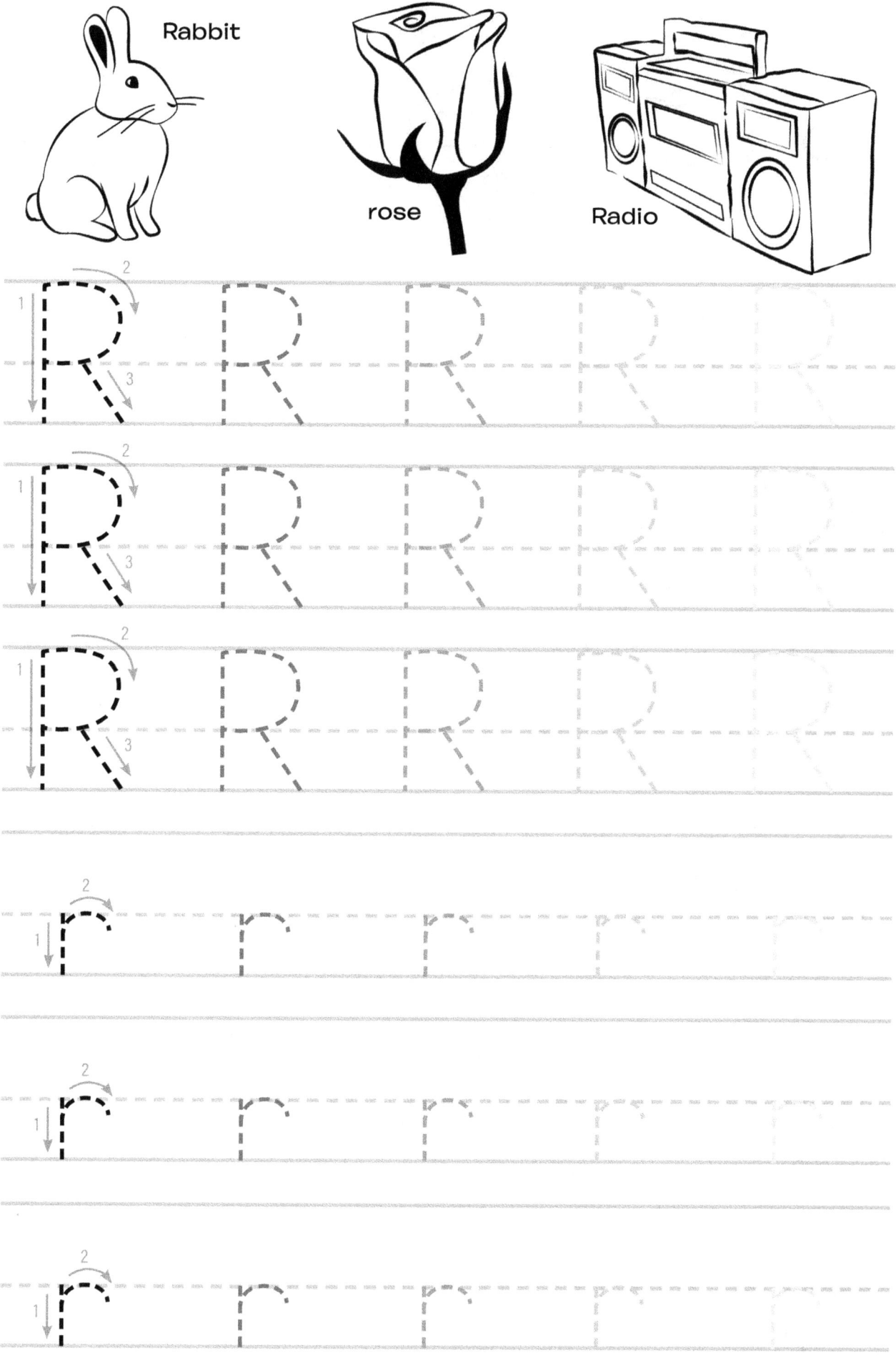

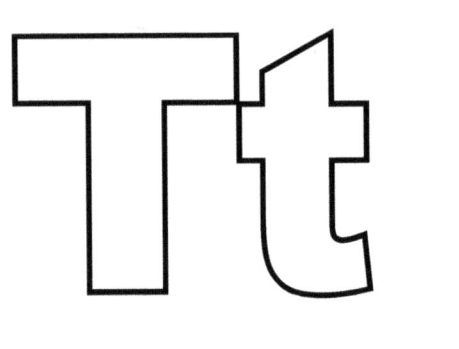

T is for top.
Trace the uppercase T and lowercase t. Color the letters and the pictures.

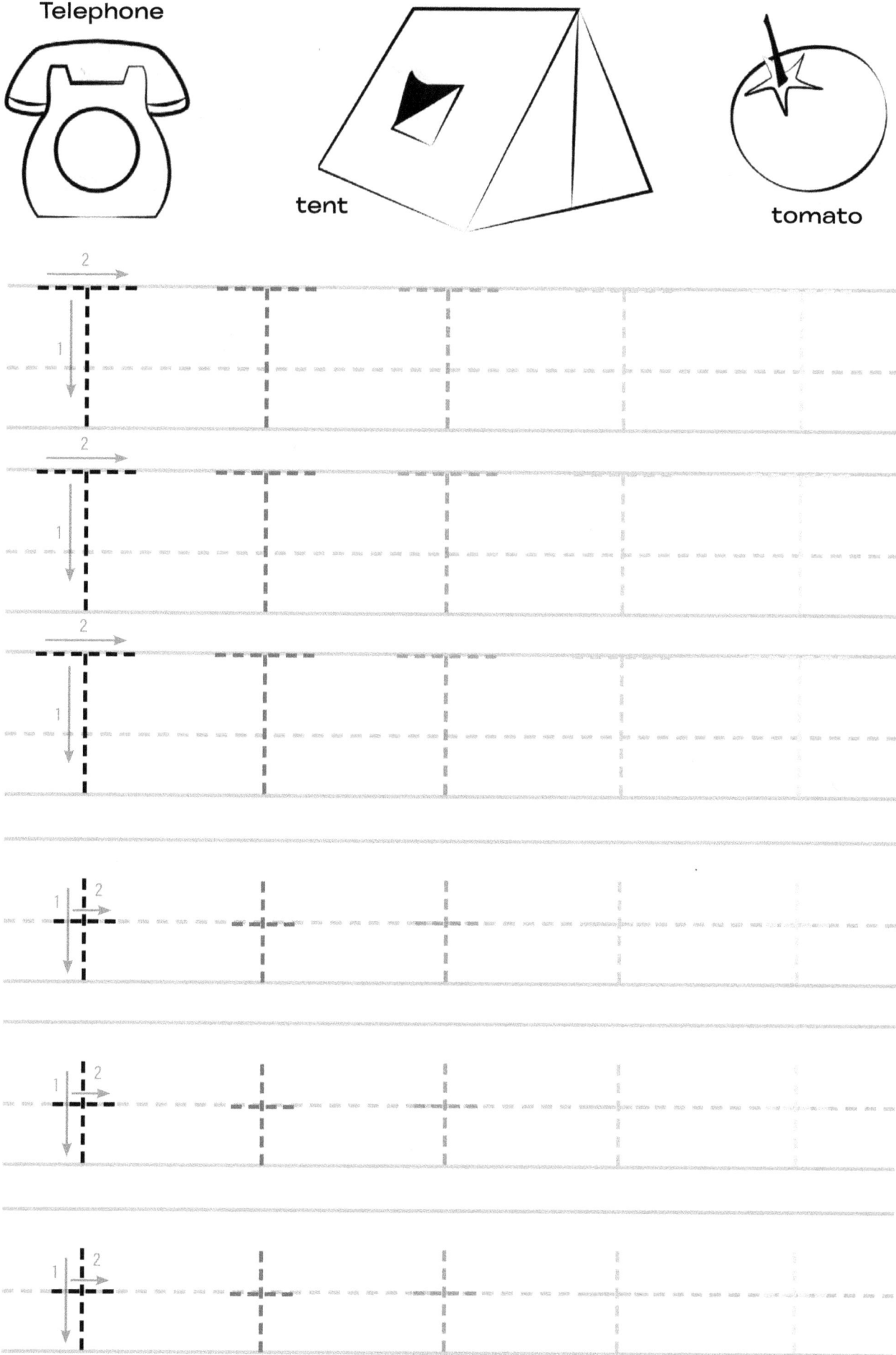

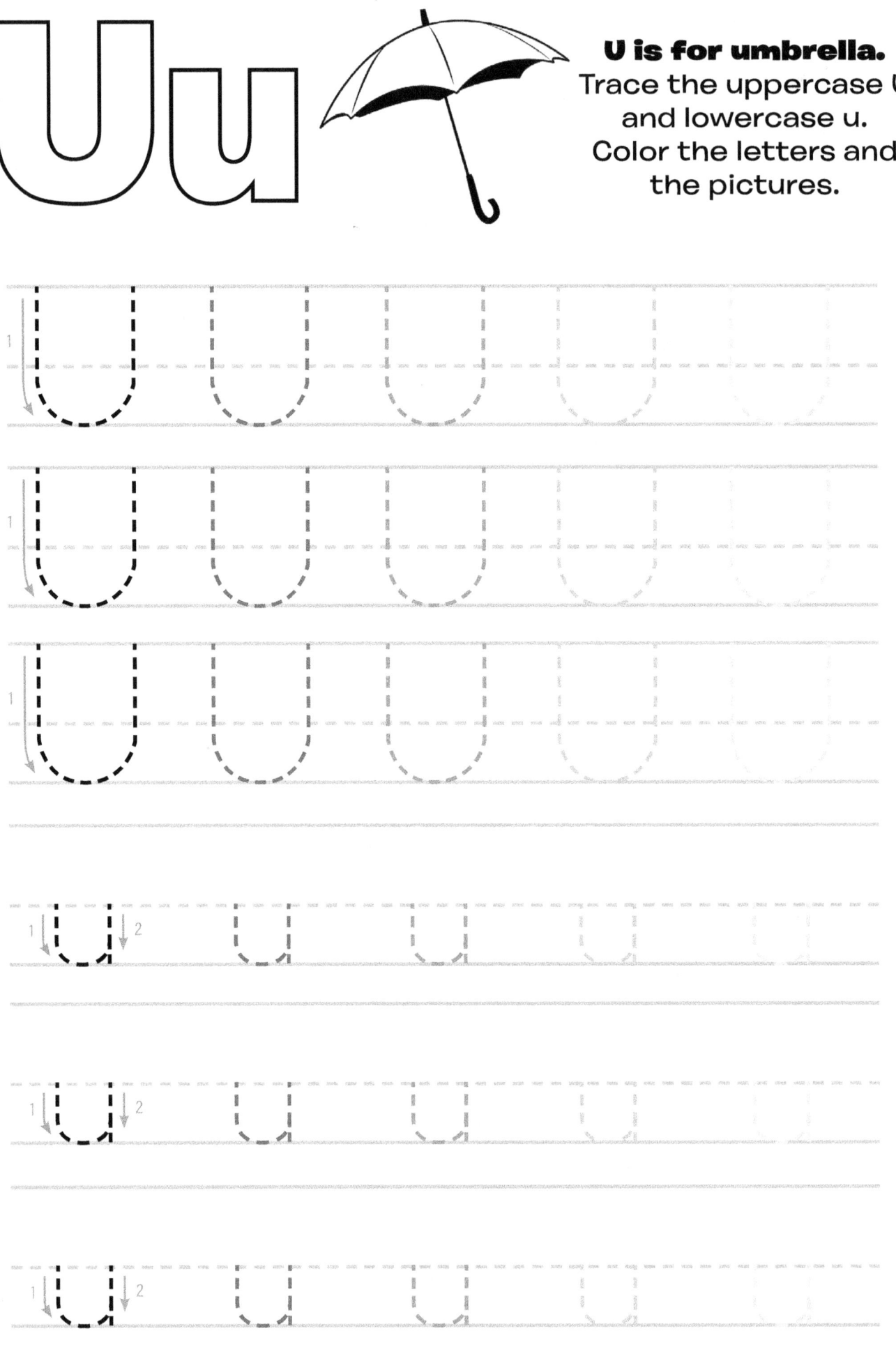

U is for umbrella.
Trace the uppercase U and lowercase u. Color the letters and the pictures.

Vv

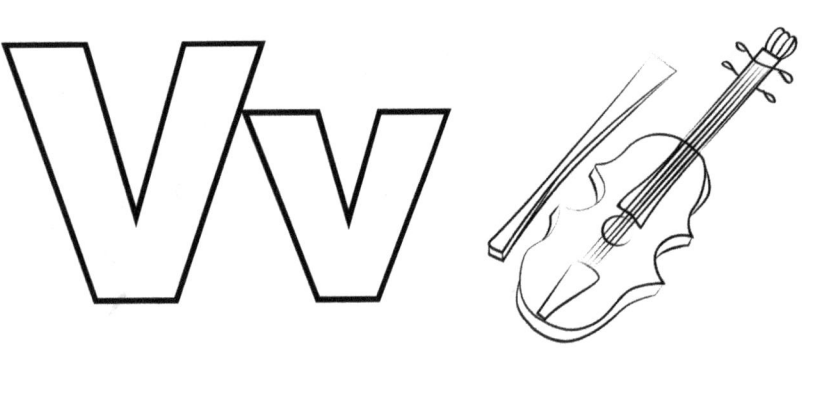

V is for violin.
Trace the uppercase V and lowercase v. Color the letters and the pictures.

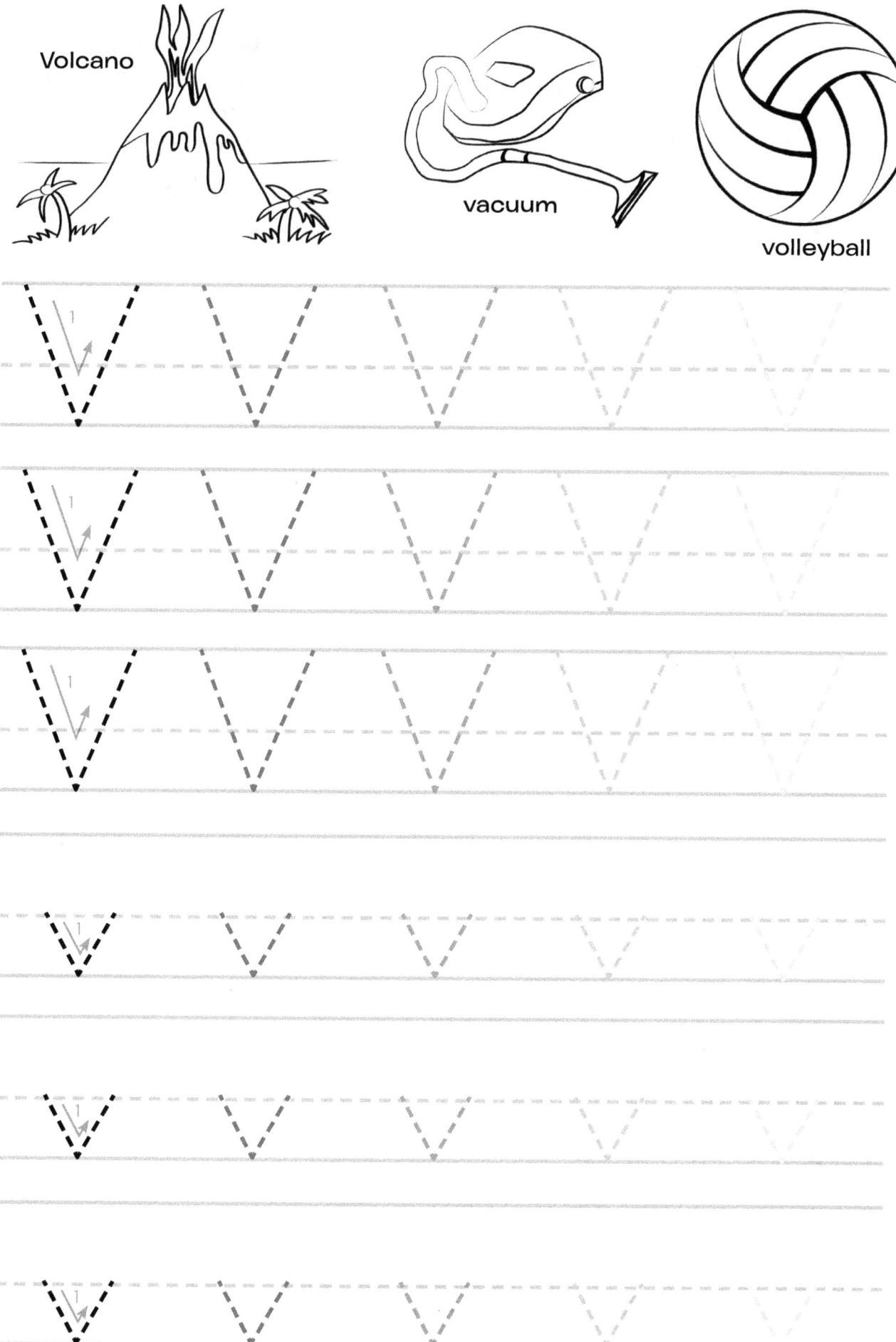

Ww

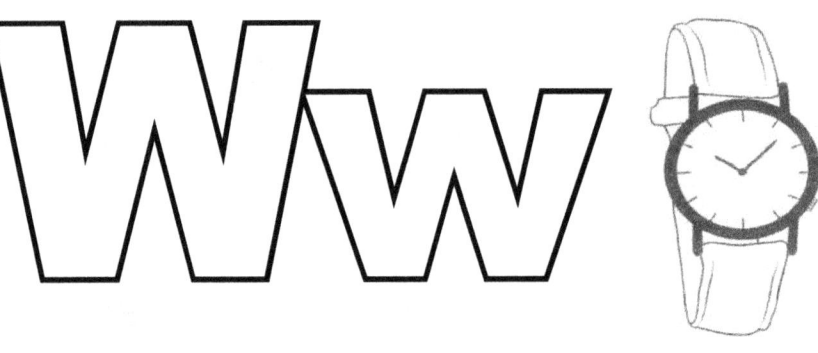

W is for watch.

Trace the uppercase W and lowercase w. Color the letters and the pictures.

Xx

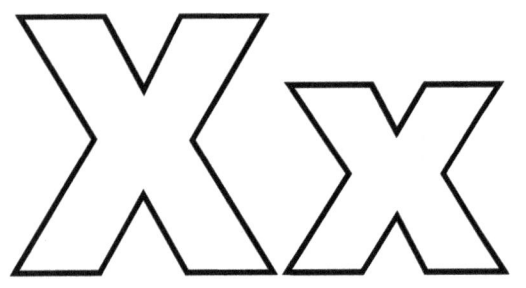

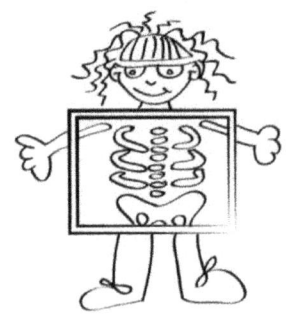

X is for x-ray.
Trace the uppercase X and lowercase x. Color the letters and the pictures.

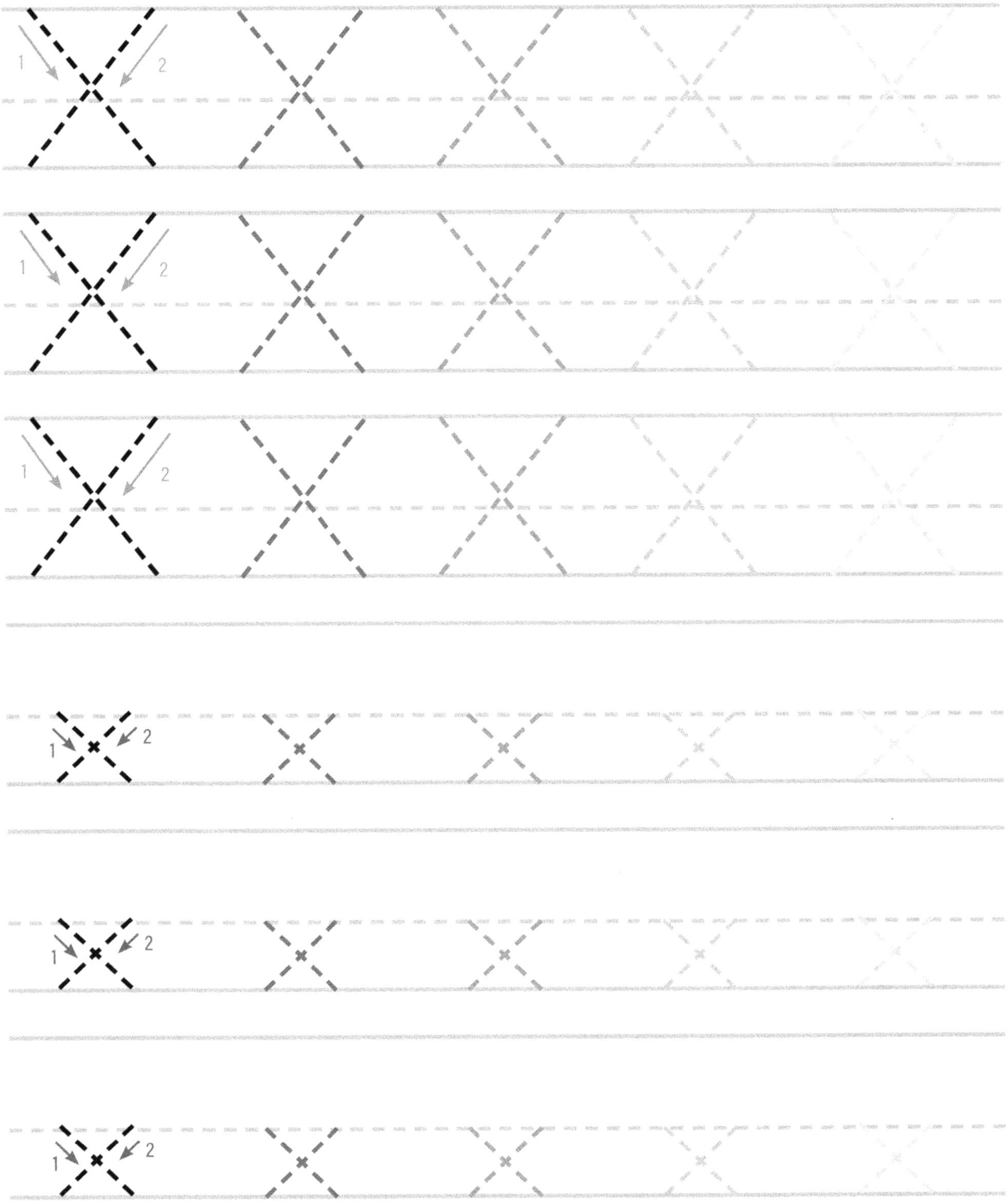

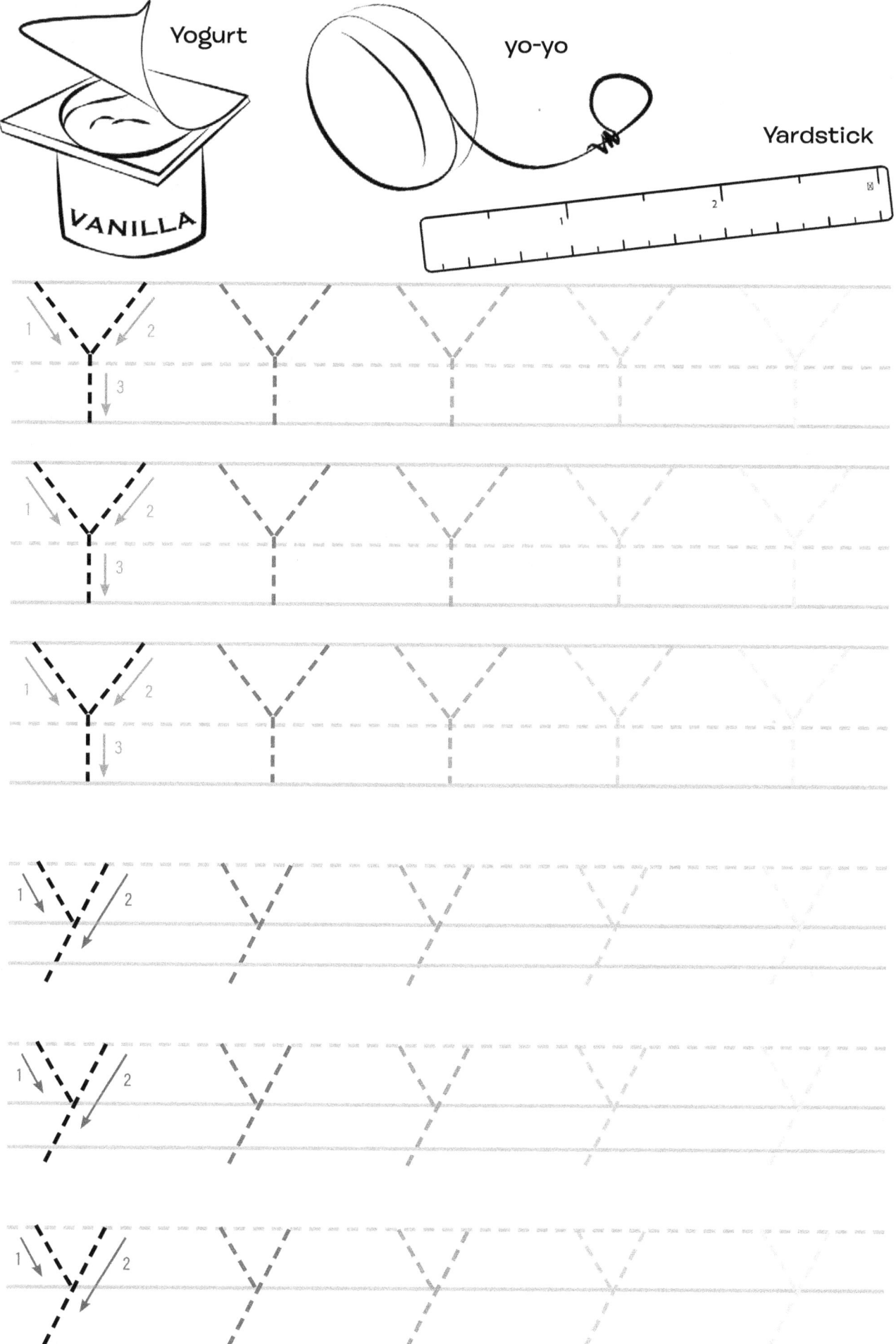

Yogurt yo-yo Yardstick

Zz

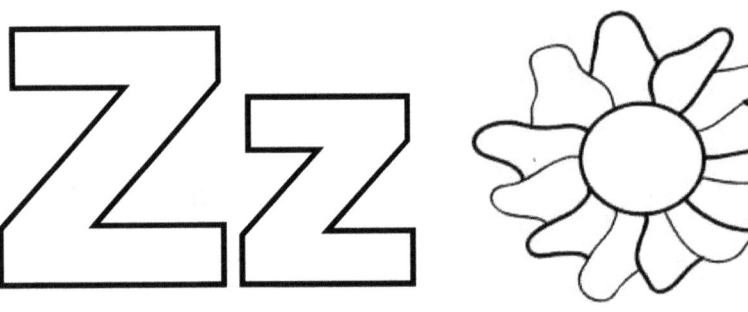

Z is for zinnia.
Trace the uppercase Z and lowercase z. Color the letters and the pictures.

zucchini zebra Zipper

Practice writing any letter or number.

Practice writing any letter or number.

Practice writing any letter or number.

Practice writing any letter or number.

Practice writing any letter or number.

Practice writing any letter or number.

Practice writing any letter or number.

Practice writing any letter or number.

Practice writing any letter or number.

Practice writing any letter or number.

Practice writing any letter or number.

Practice writing any letter or number.

Practice writing any letter or number.

Practice writing any letter or number.

Practice writing any letter or number.

Practice writing any letter or number.

Practice writing any letter or number.

Practice writing any letter or number.

Practice writing any letter or number.

Practice writing any letter or number.

Practice writing any letter or number.

Practice writing any letter or number.

Practice writing any letter or number.

Practice writing any letter or number.

Practice writing any letter or number.

Practice writing any letter or number.

Practice writing any letter or number.

Practice writing any letter or number.

Practice writing any letter or number.

Practice writing any letter or number.

Practice writing any letter or number.

Practice writing any letter or number.

Practice writing any letter or number.

Practice writing any letter or number.

Practice writing any letter or number.

Practice writing any letter or number.

Practice writing any letter or number.

Practice writing any letter or number.

Practice writing any letter or number.

Practice writing any letter or number.

www.ingramcontent.com/pod-product-compliance
Lightning Source LLC
Chambersburg PA
CBHW080523030426

42337CB00023B/4610